Further Useful Tips for Woodturners

Further Useful Tips for Woodturners

Guild of Master Craftsman Publications Ltd

This collection first published in 1999 by
Guild of Master Craftsman Publications Ltd,
Castle Place, 166 High Street, Lewes,
East Sussex BN7 1XU

© GMC Publications 1999

ISBN 1 86108 121 9

Front cover photograph by Ceri Matthews (see tip on page 13)
Illustrations by Simon Rodway

A catalogue record of this book is available from the British Library

Designed by Edward Le Froy

Printed and bound in Great Britain
by Ebenezer Baylis & Son Ltd

Contents

Techniques

Chucks

Storage

Modifying and Improving Lathes

Introduction

THE READERS' tips that we receive at the *Woodturning* office never cease to amaze me with their inventiveness, ingenuity and usefulness. In many cases they are the result of a turner being confronted with a problem or irritation, and then finding a solution. Some, such as those for storage, are applicable to most turners' workshops; others may be more specific in their application, and just what you have been looking for to solve a certain problem.

The range of the 92 tips reproduced here is really quite amazing. I have never seen another woodturners' book that talks about such things as using dental wax to seal wood, or a sweet jar as a dust extractor hood!

My thanks go out to the many readers who send in their tips to *Woodturning*; this enables us not only to pass on their ideas through the magazine, but also to reproduce them in this handy and thought-provoking volume.

Terry Porter
Former Editor, *Woodturning*

Tools & Equipment

A SIMPLE CENTRE FINDER

Here is a quick and easy way to find the centre of round or square section timber, particularly when mounting on the lathe.

All you need are three pieces of any softwood, cut to size and assembled as shown in the drawing, plus a piece of brass or similar material to act as a straightedge, screwed on the centreline of the base.

When the wood is laid on the jig, draw a line along the edge of the brass plate, then turn the timbers through 90° and draw another line. The lines will cross at the centre of the timber.

D A Richardson

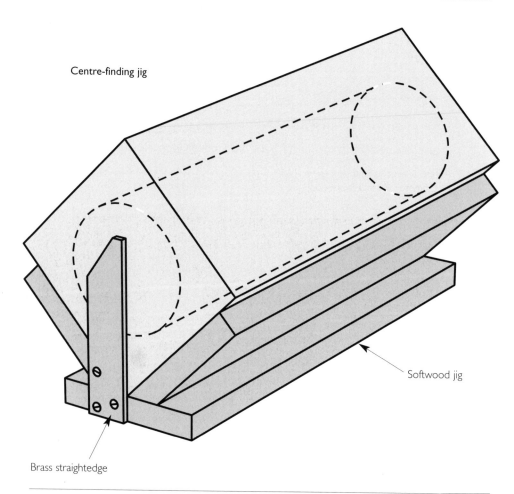

Centre-finding jig

Softwood jig

Brass straightedge

USING A WORKMATE TO HOLD BOWL AND CHUCK

I use a 'Workmate' type of bench with a ply or medium density fibreboard (MDF) top to help me when carving or shaping the tops of bowls and vases.

I erect the workbench, close the top fully and then open it 6mm (¼in). About 150mm (6in) from one end I mark a circle in the centre of the top plates, the same size as the central body of my scroll chuck (the part at the back of the chuck, where it fits on to the lathe). I cut out the circle, and the job is complete.

After turning a bowl, I remove it from the lathe with the chuck still attached, then place them in the workbench hole and tighten the clamp.

You can then sit at the end of the bench and carve or shape the top of the bowl with 360° access. And if you need to tilt the bowl to work it, a block or couple of bricks under one end of the bench does the trick.

Converting my bench was the most useful half-hour I ever spent. The normal uses of the Workmate are in no way affected.

Richard Pain

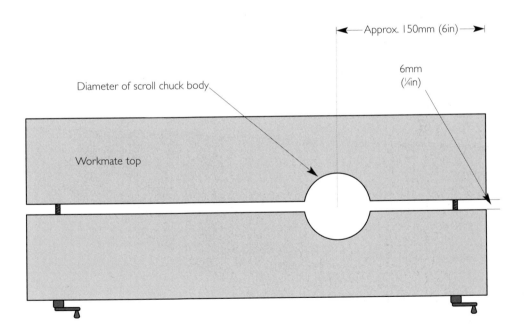

Approx. 150mm (6in)

6mm (¼in)

Diameter of scroll chuck body

Workmate top

A converted workbench

A Drive Centre for Small Pieces

My four-prong drive was too big to turn small pieces of wood to a small diameter and I solved the problem by using a drive tool like the one shown. I pressed a 16mm (⅝in) diameter head onto a standard MC1 drill chuck taper and pressed a four-prong Phillips screwdriver into the head.

I've used this drive for a long time now, and find it very satisfactory in combination with a mini revolving centre (my own development) in the tailstock.

I have also designed an MC2 drill chuck taper and threaded heads, the latter for lathe head spindles with internal screw thread, such as metric M16.

H J Van Hunen

Mini four-prong drive centre

Safety and Reading Glasses Combined

Having to wear safety glasses for protection and reading glasses to see what I was turning, brought several problems. There were, for example, twice as many surfaces to get dirty, and I had to choose safety glasses big enough to cover my reading lens without touching and scratching them. To overcome this, I decided to get some safety spectacles made to my reading glasses prescription. It took visits to two or three opticians before I found one who understood the problem and could help. The glasses I now have are both comfortable and reassuring.

Make sure your new glasses are supplied with documents showing they comply with the appropriate British or European standard. This must apply to the frame and the lens, not just the latter. The standards are BS2738 or EN166-F and equate to the old BS2092.2. The glasses must be able to withstand a cricket ball at an impact speed of 45 metres per second. To put things in perspective, a 305mm (12in) diameter bowl turning at 1,000rpm has a peripheral speed of about 15 metres per second. The price was somewhere between the special offer frame and the designer frame, but it was money well spent.

Dick Mather

(If working on the lathe, it's advisable to have the correct focal length for your glasses verified by an optician – Ed)

Threaded Rod For Accurate Tolerances

I was recently asked to turn a pair of sleeves with an internal diameter of 13mm (½in) and a wall thickness of 1.5mm (⅟₁₆in) to fit a recess. But how was I to support and turn them?

My solution was to first turn a piece of threaded rod, of 13mm (½in) diameter and get a nut to fit (a Nyloc type is best). Then I drilled a piece of hardwood two thirds deep.

The threaded rod was held in the headstock in a Jacobs chuck and the wood to be turned was drilled through and mounted on the rod. The part-drilled (pressure block) was slipped on the rod and the tailstock brought up to support the end.

Pressure was applied, the piece to support the end held firmly between the nut (which is adjustable) and the pressure block. Any rotation of the work on the rod was taken up with masking tape to ensure a snug fit. It was then turned to the required thickness.

The internal support allows turning to very accurate tolerances.

This idea can be adapted to various situations by using different sizes of threaded rods and nuts. They are fairly cheap to make.

R Vine

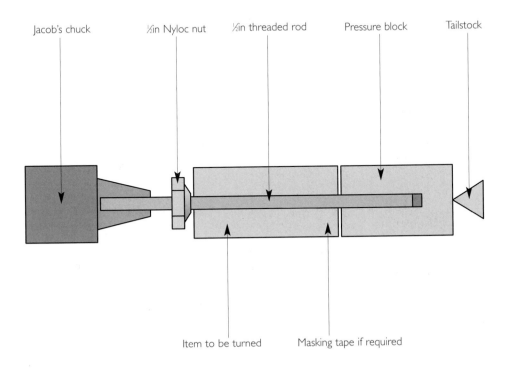

The threaded rod in place

BENCH CLAMP FOR CUTTING LOGS

Trying to build up my wood stock, I used a wooden horse for cutting logs into usable sizes with the Bosch Tyrannosaw. But how to cut logs into billets in a safe and secure way became a problem.

The bench clamp shown works well for this (*see illustrations below and on facing page*). It can also be used for cutting by hand or power saw.

As I work at an oil refinery, getting scrap for my clamp was easy, but most engineering firms should be able to supply the parts.

Roger Arnott

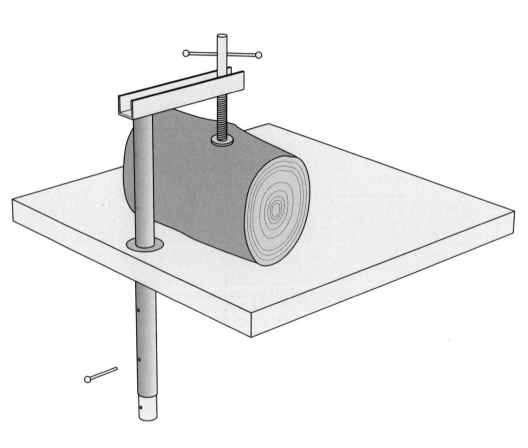

Roger Arnott's bench clamp

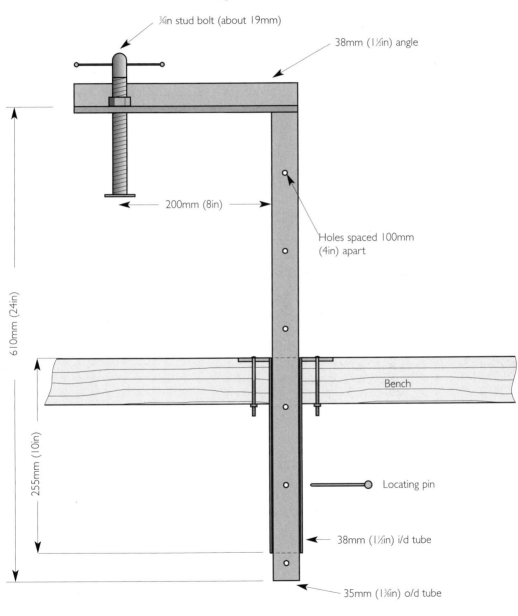

¾in stud bolt (about 19mm)

38mm (1½in) angle

200mm (8in)

Holes spaced 100mm (4in) apart

610mm (24in)

255mm (10in)

Bench

Locating pin

38mm (1½in) i/d tube

35mm (1⅜in) o/d tube

Hand Guard for Spiralling Tool

A possible shortcoming with the Robert Sorby texturing and spiralling system is that, while it is extremely well engineered, the hand nearest the cutting wheel can easily slide forward along the smooth bar and come uncomfortably close to the cutter.

To prevent my fingers becoming spiralled, I devised a simple guard. It can be made in under an hour, requires no alteration to the tool, and completely protects the hand. (*See illustrations below and on facing page.*)

G H Anson

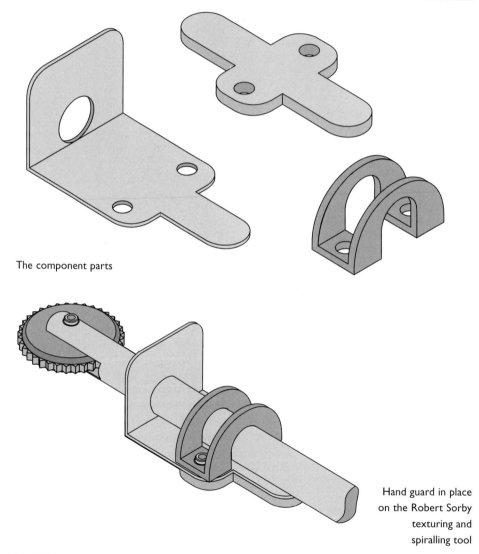

The component parts

Hand guard in place
on the Robert Sorby
texturing and
spiralling tool

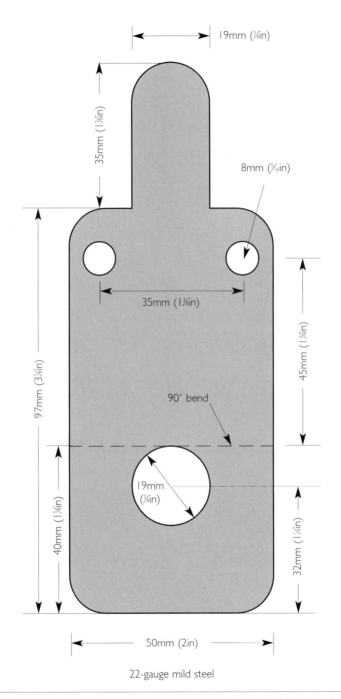

19mm (¾in)

35mm (1⅜in)

8mm (⁵⁄₁₆in)

35mm (1⅜in)

45mm (1¾in)

90° bend

97mm (3⅞in)

19mm
(¾in)

40mm (1⅝in)

32mm (1¼in)

50mm (2in)

22-gauge mild steel

CHISEL GRINDING MADE EASY

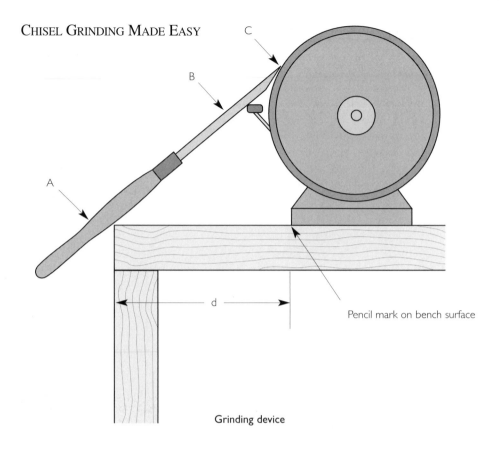

Pencil mark on bench surface

Grinding device

I've developed a method of getting an accurate and repeatable edge to a chisel, without using special equipment. My grinding wheel is bolted to a wooden base, which is free to be moved anywhere on the top surface of the bench.

For each chisel there is a particular distance of the grinding wheel from the edge of the bench (distance 'd' in the illustration), which gives the chisel the following three points of fixed support:
i) The chisel handle, with the bench edge (point A)
ii) The chisel's shaft, with the wheel's rest (point B)
iii) The chisel's edge, with the wheel (point C)
When the wheel is moved to roughly its correct position on the bench, the chisel is placed on points A and B, and gently eased up until its edge touches the wheel at point C.

You get the edge profile you want by moving the wheel slightly towards or away from the bench edge and, when satisfied, starting the wheel and sharpening the chisel.

After completion, a pencil-line can be drawn on the bench along the edge of the wheel's base, to ensure that the next time you want to sharpen the chisel, you can do so with minimum grinding.

Eric Ballard

TURNING FERRULES TRUE ON A TURNERS' LATHE

Percy Blandford has described how you can turn the ends of the ferrule true, when making sound hardwood handles for your turning tools, if you have a metalworking lathe or can hold the tube in a chuck on your woodturning lathe. But what if you haven't?

I have a metalworking lathe in my workshop, but my simple three-jaw self-centring chuck can't properly grip thin wall pipes. So I make my ferrules on a woodworking lathe.

First, I turn a wooden spindle, of the same diameter as the inside of the pipe, then I put the pipe on to a stick and use a screw to lock it in place.

Lastly, I cut ferrules with a tool similar to the HSS diamond-point scraper, though holding a hacksaw on the rotating tube may be safer for beginners.

Andrew Naczynski

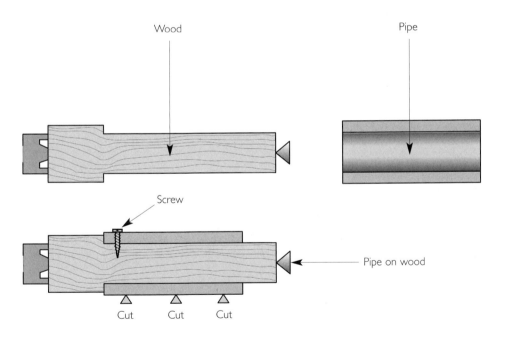

Wood

Pipe

Screw

Pipe on wood

Cut   Cut   Cut

LIGHTWEIGHT FOLDING WORK TABLE

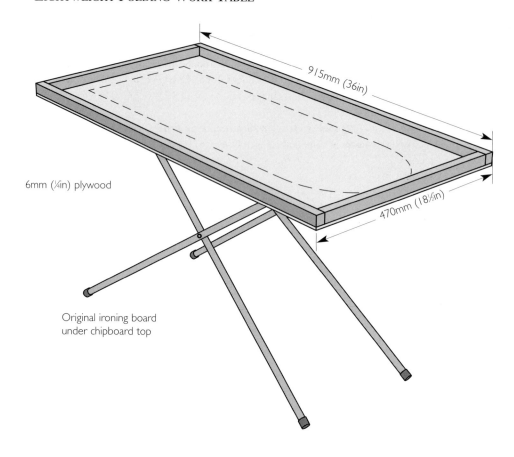

915mm (36in)

6mm (¼in) plywood

470mm (18½in)

Original ironing board
under chipboard top

Ironing board converted into foldaway work table

With a few modifications, a redundant ironing board is transformed into a lightweight foldaway work table.

The ironing board I used had a chipboard top, so my extended top was screwed directly to this. Ironing boards with metal tops would need a different fitting, perhaps self-tapping screws.

I find this work table invaluable for keeping tools and accessories in one place, immediately to hand. Gone are those frustrating moments when items you want to use seem to have disappeared into thin air.

This table has the added advantage that it neatly folds away when not in use.

R W Warnham

Ball-ended Handle Gives More Control

I have recently looked at better control of my woodturning chisels, my fingers having become stiffer over the past few years.

For an improved grip and the sensitive control needed in woodturning, I tried inlaying a few 'O' rings into the handles at certain points – some factory-made handles have decorative grooves cut into their handles which, with a little deepening, will take a few 'O' rings without much trouble. Ever cost-conscious, I also tried putting masking tape around the handle at essential points. All this improved grip and control.

But I like to make my own handles and to experiment with their shape. The best shape for me, so far, has been the development of what I can only call my finger and thumb ring, which sits just behind the ferrule. This shape allows me to rest my thumb or wrap my finger around the handle, improving grip and control.

The illustration shows one example – an ash handle for a bowl finishing scraper. It is 440mm (17⅜in) long (big enough to dampen vibration), with a maximum diameter of 40mm (1⅝in) and with nearly 45mm (1¾in) diameter for the support ring and the ball end. The ferrule is brass (I hate copper pipe, finding it too soft) and the finish is Liberon's finishing oil. This gives a finish with a positive, tactile surface.

The ball end is comfortable to handle and will not slip through stiff fingers in the way narrow-ended factory handles can. It also helps indicate handle positioning, against the body or in the hand, while turning.

This shape works for me, but experiment with the size and position of the finger and thumb ring to suit your own grip.

Ceri Matthews

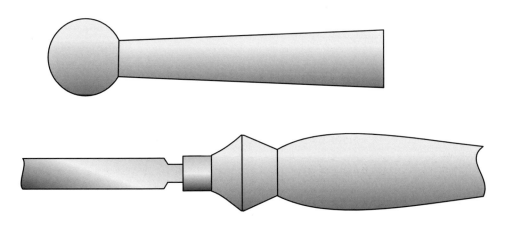

The ball-ended tool handle, with finger and thumb ring just behind the ferrule

COLLAPSIBLE SEAT FOR BACK SUFFERERS

I suffer from a back problem which forces me to sit down often. As my workshop is tiny, I devised a collapsible seat which takes up very little room when collapsed.

The illustration on the facing page gives the dimensions, but the height can be adjusted to make it comfortable for the user.

Ian Burrell

EFFECTIVE BENCH HOOK FOR SORBY PROFILING JIG

I recommend the excellent Robert Sorby 445 Fingernail Profiling Jig, and have made a small bench hook to set the 50mm (2in) projection of the gouge from the jig.

This is simply a piece of 12mm (½in) ply, 50 x 71mm (2 x 2¹³⁄₁₆in) with two pieces of 50 x 20 x 20mm (2 x ¾ x ¾in) plywood attached to it. The hardwood is faced with laminate to give a harder-wearing surface.

To use, the bench hook is put on the edge of a bench, either way up, and the gouge and profiling jig set to it. Its simple, effective, and gives the same projection every time.

Gavin Chapman

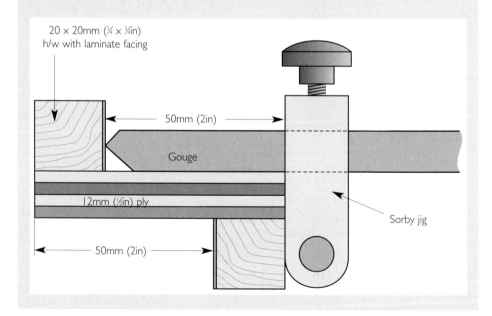

20 x 20mm (¾ x ¾in)
h/w with laminate facing

50mm (2in)

Gouge

12mm (½in) ply

50mm (2in)

Sorby jig

Side view of the seat when collapsed

125mm (5in)

Plan view

268mm (10½in)

125mm (5in)

25mm
(1in)

418mm (16½in)

Existing wooden
bench pillar

673mm (26½in)

267mm (10½in)

Side view
in use

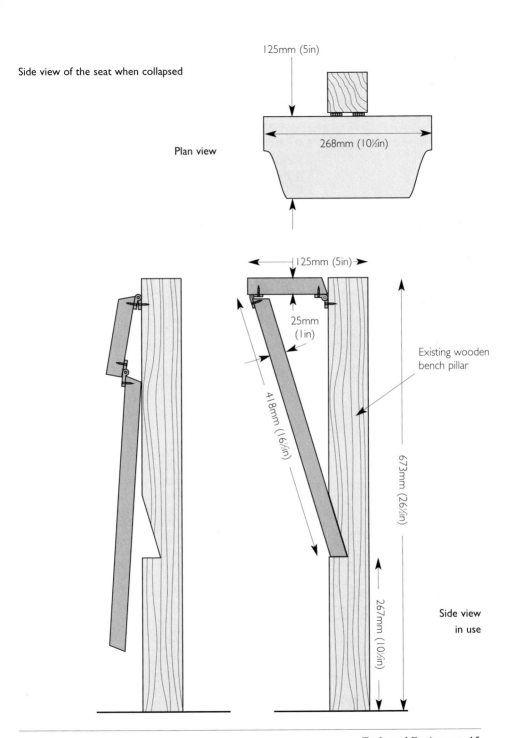

A Handle for Holding Small, Light Tools

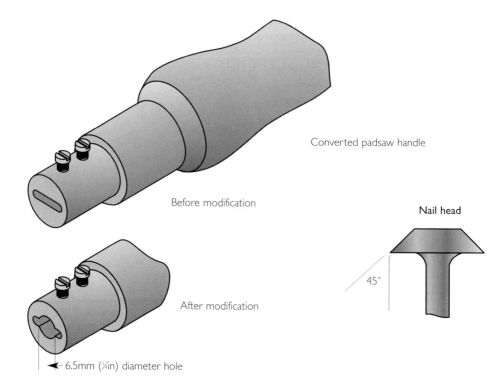

Converted padsaw handle

Before modification

After modification

6.5mm (¼in) diameter hole

Nail head

45°

1 Remove collar from handle
2 Using a pillar drill and vice, drill the 6.5mm (¼in) diameter hole
3 With a V-block, open up the two remaining screw holes, and tap to take grub screws (socket head)
4 Re-assemble collar to handle and run 6.5mm drill through collar again and into the handle, to allow the tool to be deeply sunk

A useful handle for holding small, home-made turning tools, can be created from a pad 'keyhole' saw handle. These can be bought quite cheaply from most DIY stores.

The grub screws used grip tighter than the existing screws, and are neater and less likely to catch on fingers or toolrests.

A useful first tool can be made from a large 160mm (6in) nail, or round-headed coach bolt. Grind a 45° chamfer to the base of the head, as shown. It behaves like a ring tool and is great for hollowing the insides of small boxes.

B R Stephens

Hacksaw Hand Tool for Cutting Studs

Cutting off studs is always a nuisance, as even flexible saws need a lot of care and the use of both hands to avoid scratching.

My answer is to make a hand tool from a fine hacksaw blade. It can be held in one hand, leaving the other free to control the tool or to support the work. Either way, by working quickly round the stud, it comes off cleanly with minimal risk of adjacent scratching.

The blade can be attached with the teeth either side, should the user be left-handed. A small hole in the end will ensure that the tool always hangs where it's needed.

Jack Ricketts

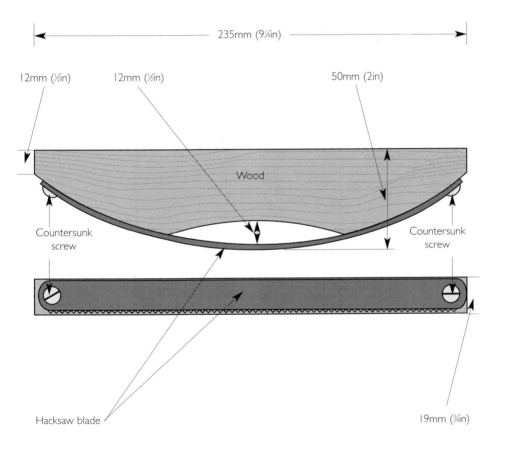

235mm (9¼in)

12mm (½in)

12mm (½in)

50mm (2in)

Wood

Countersunk screw

Countersunk screw

Hacksaw blade

19mm (¾in)

Stud-removing tool

Making Your Own Gouge-grinding Jig

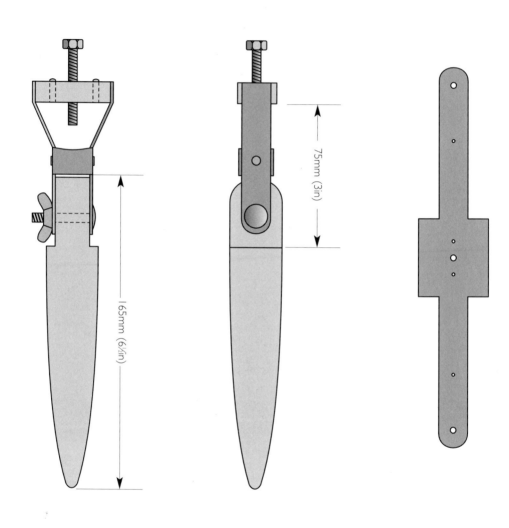

The home-made gouge-grinding jig

Several jigs have recently come onto the market for grinding gouges but, as a pensioner who turns for pleasure, I did not want the expense of buying one, so decided to make my own.

The shaft is turned from oak, with a small flat on the top end, and the strap from sheet steel about 1mm (⅜in) thick, which is easily bent to the required shape.

I riveted a small piece of mild steel in the top of the strap, drilled and tapped to take a small bolt. Alternatively, you could use a nut and suitable adhesive.

A small, hardwood block is held in place with a small nut and bolt to form a bed on which the gouge sits. This block is slightly recessed on each side, and the metal strap fits into these recesses, so keeping the block from twisting out of position. This is a better arrangement than having several screws or bolts in a small wooden block.

The bolt and wing-nut hold the two parts of the jig together and enable the jig to be set up for grinding.

My two-wheel Black & Decker grinder sits on a small shelf in the garage, where space is at a premium. So I have a wooden arm bolted under the shelf which swings out when needed.

I use the most suitable of the small, blind holes in the arm to hold the tapered end of the jig. It's simple to set up and the results are very satisfactory.

I made the jig from materials and scrap to hand. The shaft length shown in the drawing could be adjusted to suit any set-up.

Roy Brown

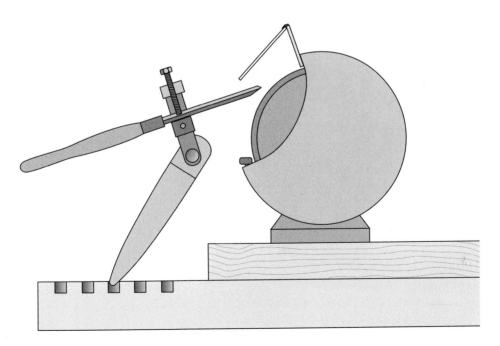

The method of operation. Note the blind holes in which to sit the base of the jig

Simple Adapter to a Sealant Gun

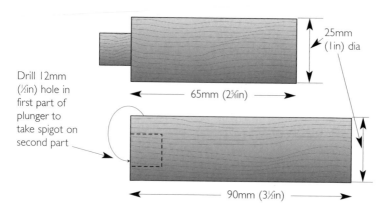

Drill 12mm (½in) hole in first part of plunger to take spigot on second part

25mm (1in) dia

65mm (2⅝in)

90mm (3½in)

Two part plunger

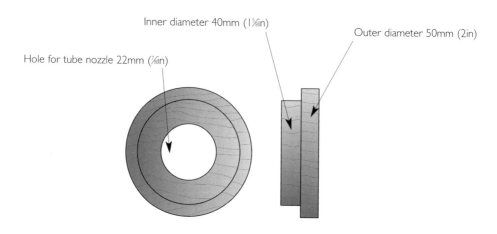

Inner diameter 40mm (1⅝in)

Outer diameter 50mm (2in)

Hole for tube nozzle 22mm (⅞in)

Side and front view of the disc

As a hobby woodturner I use Craft Supplies' silicone sealant to stick ceramic tiles to wood surrounds, but find the plastic plunger difficult to push by hand. To solve this problem I adapted my industrial-size sealant gun to take the 75ml tube by making three simple scrap wood turnings.

First I turned a disc to fit in the front of the gun, then a plunger in two parts. I can now use the gun for both sizes of tube.

J C Elsom

HOLDING WOOD STEADY FOR CHAINSAWING

To hold logs steady when chainsawing them into bowl blanks, I first cut a 50mm (2in) deep slot with the chain saw, lengthways. The slot will be vertical when the log is stood on its end grain.

To give ground clearance and improve stability, I then nail two 50 x 50mm (2 x 2in) battens in a V shape to the base.

An F-cramp can be fitted into the slot with its head under the log and the free end screwed down onto the blank to hold it firm, as the illustration shows. Take care to keep the chainsaw clear of the metal clamp, for safety.

P J Smith

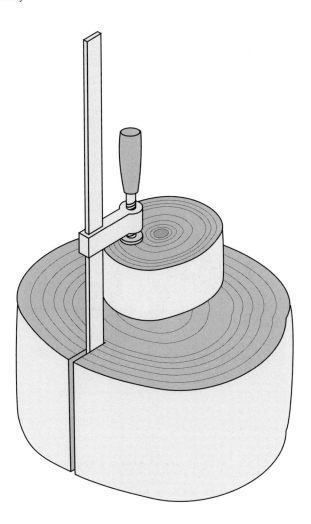

A device for sawing logs safely with a chainsaw

A ROTATING STAND FOR TWIST DRILLS

I often use engineers' twist drills for drilling small holes on my turners' lathe, and store 19 drills in a proprietary circular stand. This can get in the way, and be knocked over, spilling drills everywhere.

I have solved this problem by bolting the stand to an arm that can be swung away from the lathe. I have also interposed a ball bearing unit between arm and drill stand, which means I can spin the stand around to find the drill I want (*see illustration below*).

I used scrap wood to make the rotating drill stand, at the heart of which is an old ball bearing unit which fitted a 25mm (1in) diameter shaft. I made a stepped wooden plug, with a clearance hole along its length, to take an 8mm (⅜in) diameter bolt. Then I drilled the stand at its centre to allow a bolt of the same size to pass through the stand and wooden plug in the ball bearing unit.

Finally, I bolted it tightly, with a nut and large washer clamped against the ball bearing inner race. The clamp round the ball bearing was bent from an odd piece of mild steel, about 2.5mm (⅟₁₆in) thick. The arm was once part of a folding deck chair and the angle piece part of an old bed.

If a stand for larger drills is wanted, it would have to be fairly thick to keep the drills upright. It could be a sandwich of wood and plywood, to save on weight and materials. The wood separating the plywood need only be of sufficient size to reinforce the holes for drills etc. and the central hole big enough for the bolt to clamp the stand to the ball bearing unit.

Derek C K Pearce

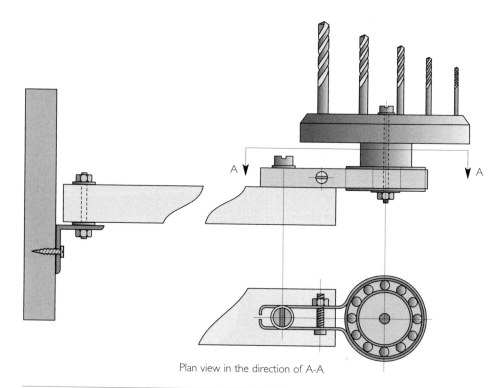

Plan view in the direction of A-A

Paint Handle Tops

Some people turn tool handles in different woods so that they can recognise the tool by the handle. Another method is to paint the end of each handle a different colour, or combination of colours.

F R Nunn

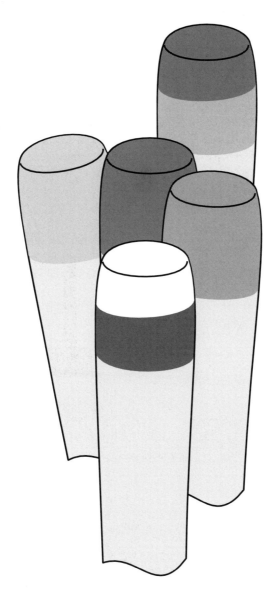

Tool handles painted to aid recognition

SMALL FOUR-PRONG DRIVE

I often need to turn small pieces of wood down to about 10mm (⅜in) or even 5mm (³⁄₁₆in) diameter, and find that my four-prong drive is too big.

I overcame this problem by putting a Phillips screwdriver bit into my four-jaw engineering chuck. This makes a nice, small, four-prong drive.

Roger Hurley

A SAWHORSE FOR RIPSAWING AND CROSS CUTTING

Here is a design for a sawhorse suitable for woodturners needing to balance logs for ripsawing with chainsaws, as well as cross cutting. I made it from 75 x 50mm (3 x 2in) softwood section, taken from an old pallet. Any other size of section would do, but it would mean adjusting the size of the matrix for peg holes.

I've used only six renewable vertical struts, as they can be renewed as they become damaged. But, with care, they should last a long time. You only need to nail the base together around the edges, working up layer by layer from the bottom, staggering the nails slightly to avoid hitting the one below. There are no nails in the sawing area.

When assembling the base, make the spaces at least 5mm (³⁄₁₆in) bigger both ways than the log support struts, to allow for swelling when wet.

This holding device is as useful for cross cutting as it is for ripsawing (*see illustration on facing page*).

Hugh Simpson

FINDING ABRASIVES

I buy cloth-backed abrasive in one-metre by 400mm (39 x 16in) lengths and in four grades. I avoid the problem of distinguishing between grades after cutting short lengths, as follows.

I lay new strips face down and, with a felt-tipped pen, mark a series of lines along the backing cloth – one line for coarse, and two, three and four lines for successive grades.

The grade of any piece can then easily be found simply by looking at the number of lines on the back of the cloth.

Norman Bastiani

Sawhorse for chainsawing, made from an old pallet

Techniques

MAKE SAVINGS ON EXOTICS

After parting off work from a spigot turned for gripping in my chuck, I swing the toolrest around, face off the end of the spigot and incise a few rings onto it. I can glue small pieces of exotic woods to the spigot and turn them (the rings help centre the blanks). This saves waste when parting the exotics, as I cut into the spigot and take only a few shavings from the expensive exotics.

P Ling

ENLARGE A SPIGOT

When turning a spigot, have you ever turned a little too much off, after spending a lot of time on the rest of the piece? Well, here's a method to overcome this problem. Coat the outside of the spigot with superglue and roll it in sawdust. Within seconds you will have a better fit.

M A C Kipping

HOT GLUE HOLDS ALUMINIUM SPIGOTS

I use a hot-melt glue to attach an aluminium spigot plate to turning blanks. To make a spigot plate, I use 10mm (⅜in) aluminium plate, from a scrap dealer.

Draw a circle to suit the jaws of your chuck (I use 75mm, 3in), and drill a 6mm (¼in) hole in the centre. Cut out the circle with a saw, or by drilling, then put a 6mm (¼in) nut and bolt through the hole so you can hold it in a Jacob's chuck on the lathe. Bring a live tail centre up for support to stop the chuck coming loose in the Morse taper.

Turn the disc to size using HSS tools at your lowest speed, then cut a step or dovetail to suit your chuck. I used a 6mm (¼in) HSS parting tool, but a scraper might be easier (you can't use gouges).

To attach the plate to a blank, place a few beads of hot-melt glue on the plate, put it in position and apply pressure with a hot iron. Clean paper between iron and plate reduces strife if you're using the household iron.

When the plate has settled into place, remove the hot iron and let the plate cool. You can now mount the blank in the chuck and get turning. To remove the spigot plate, simply heat it again with the iron. Glue traces are removed with a cabinet scraper. If a blank does not have a flat area to mount the spigot plate on, mount the piece in a jam chuck, turn a flat, put some beads of hot-melt on the flat, then position the spigot plate. While the glue is still hot, I bring up the tailstock with a conical live centre and push this into the centre hole of the plate. Rotating the lathe by hand centralises the plate. Leave the tail centre in place until the glue has set, then you can remount the work in the chuck.

Doug Birchall

Spindle Thread Protection

I use a short length of Polypipe to protect the spindle thread on my Myford Mystro lathe. It only requires a slight shaving of the internal bore at one end (to allow for the nose register), to make it a secure push fit over the thread.

As the pipe is plastic it does not rust or bind on the thread and, unlike the purpose-made metal protector, has the added advantage that, if the cutting edge accidentally hits the Polypipe, the edge is not damaged.

The Myford Mystro has a spindle nose thread of 1⅛in x 12 tpi, and a nose register of 1¼in (approx. 32mm) diameter. I find the 1³⁄₁₆in internal bore Polypipe ideal for the job. I'm sure this type of protection could be used for other makes of lathe, using a section of Polypipe of the appropriate diameter.

R Warnham

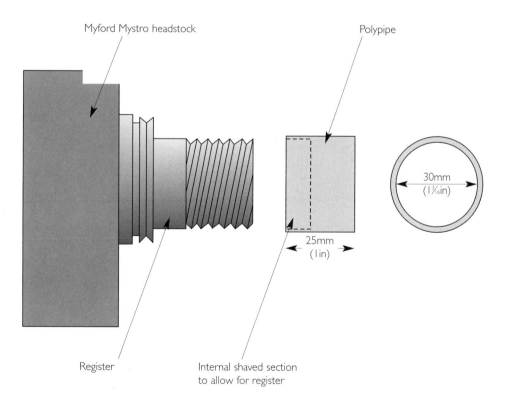

Myford Mystro headstock

Polypipe

30mm
(1³⁄₁₆in)

25mm
(1in)

Register

Internal shaved section
to allow for register

Spindle nose thread protector

Dental Wax is Good for Sealing Wood

As an alternative to sealing wax for end grain etc., call on your local dental laboratory and ask for their waste wax. They will be only too happy to get rid of it.

Melt the wax in an old baking tray, taking care not to boil or spill it. Dip end grain, or anything else which needs sealing, into this.

I've used this method for some time, with only the odd piece splitting. It's perfect if you have a lot of timber to seal, especially if it's free.

Paul Jordan

Pads to Prevent Burnt Fingers when Sanding

I have come up with the following solution to prevent burnt fingers when sanding. Simply buy a pack of Scotch Brite pads, which cost from 10p to 35p for the more racy, executive models. Cut a pad to the required size and fold the sandpaper around it.

Hey presto! You now own a technologically-advanced and effective Heat Dissipation Unit (HDU) that prevents nasty, irritating burns and moulds itself to the shape of the sanded item. It's particularly useful when sanding with fine grades of wet and dry.

Russell Dodgson

Sponges to Apply Finish Stay in Jar

As a woodturner, I use many types of finishing materials, sanding sealer, oils, stains and polyurethane, usually in small amounts.

An applicator can be costly to buy and time-consuming to clean, so I make my own. I cut a 25mm (1in) square piece of foam sponge (the type used in foam brushes) and hold it with surgical forceps bought at a flea market.

Once finished with, I drop the sponge in the can of finish, where it stays until the next application.

Now, all my cans of finish have a small piece of foam sponge inside, waiting to coat the next bowl or candlestick.

Bob Edwards

Drill Bit Cleaner

I have recently turned pens. To speed the cleaning of the drill bit, which I have glued into a home-made handle, I hold a wax candle in my left hand and when I withdraw the drill bit from the wood, wipe off the swarf with the candle.

Two wipes and it is clean. And it is lubricated for the next cut.

Peter Baker

FACEPLATE JIG

To centre your faceplate ring to a bowl blank, cut a wooden disc and screw in a hook or eye until the point protrudes on the other side. This can then be slotted into the compass-point mark on the blank.

It is far easier than looking for a rule or tape. When you've finished with the jig, simply hang it on a hook for the next time.

J Chard

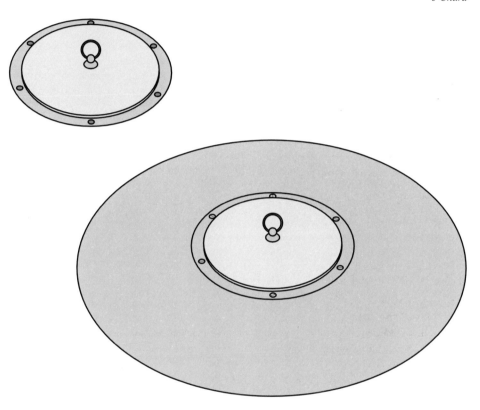

Faceplate jig

A SMOOTHER TOOLREST

For a perfectly smooth toolrest, before each turning session rub the rest with fine grinding paste on a cloth, and buff with a clean cloth.

T Gray

The Many Uses of Masking Tape

Masking tape has many uses for turners. I use it on pummels (the square part left on chair and table legs to receive the mortice joints). Wrapping tape around the cutting line stops the corners splitting.

I also use masking tape when making natural-edged bowls, winding tape around the wavy edge before cutting out the inside. This gives a positive sight-line instead of ghosting, and helps prevent me catching my fingers.

Putting tape around a drill bit or a long-hole borer serves as an indicator of depth.

When box making, I wrap tape around the lid joint to hold the lid on, while the box is held in the chuck. This allows me to clean up the top of the lid on the lathe with light cuts.

If the lid is a loose fit, I wrap tape around the rebate before putting the lid on the box for cleaning up.

I also use masking tape to fix bowls to jam chucks, as an extra safety precaution.

George Karon

Shoelace Solution

I was recently too generous in providing a rebate for my expanding chuck jaws, which left them far too loose. Rather than using a rag or wood shavings to fill the gap, I used a round shoelace. This was cut to the size of the circumference and slotted neatly into the rebate dovetail. It worked a treat.

Peter Hallam

Oil Stone Cleaner

To clean oil stones, slip stones and diamond stones of oil and grime, try using Blackfriars Paintklenz. You will be amazed at how they clean up as good as new, with a perfect surface.

T Gray

Waxing Log Ends to Prevent Splits

A quick and easy way of waxing the cut ends of logs to prevent them splitting during storage is as follows. First, prop the log so that the cut end is horizontal. Then, with a candle in one hand and a butane torch in the other, melt the end of the candle and rub it over the log with the flame still playing upon it. If the candle grease lights, it can be easily blown out.

Candle stumps can be held in pliers, or placed on the log end and melted, the wax being painted into the wood with a longer candle.

This process gives a good, even, seal, since the wood will dry out under the melted wax. You might think it sounds hazardous, but it isn't. Try it. It takes about 30 seconds to wax a 200mm (8in) log end.

Dr B W Langley

STICKY SOLUTION

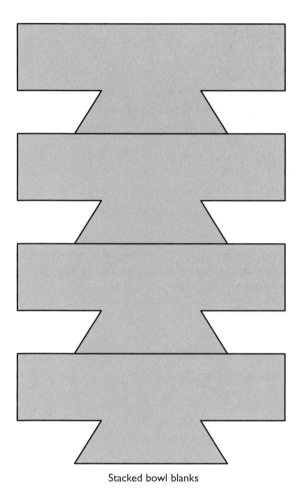

Stacked bowl blanks

After slicing logs and cutting bowl blanks, seal the edges with waterproof PVA. Leave the blanks for six months, which is when the most movement takes place. Mount the blank on the lathe and true both sides and the edge. Cut the dovetail to suit your chuck, and then reseal the edges with the glue.

This process has several advantages. For example, any cracks on the edges can be turned out, leaving a slightly smaller blank. You can also see the grain better when choosing bowl blanks, and if stacked on top of each other they will store tidily and dry better (*see illustration above*).

T Gray

Long Hole Boring Tailstock

Instead of spending a large sum on a long hole boring kit, I decided to make my own tailstock device and use a long pattern drill instead of an auger (*see illustration on facing page*).

The tailstock jig consists of a length of tableleg, 63mm (2½in) square, with a spigot turned at one end to fit into the toolrest saddle – obviously, with the toolrest removed.

On each of the four faces, at centre height, I have drilled holes with Forstner bits, about 6mm (¼in) deep, to take a spigot on the piece to be bored. A 10mm (⅜in) hole drilled right through the centres takes the long pattern drill.

The recesses on each face are of different sizes to cater for different projects.

To turn, say, a table lamp, I start between centres and turn the necessary spigot and recess at one end to use the PCC2000 three-way split ring and a 25mm (1in) spigot at the other to fit the tailstock jig.

I use the three-way split ring because it is a solid way of holding, and because there is a hole through the centre which allows (if you don't wander) for a single boring operation.

With the workpiece in the PCC2000, the tailstock jig is inserted into the toolrest saddle and fitted to the spigot. The latter has been waxed with Liberon Woodturners' Stick to ease friction.

An advantage of this system is that the auger (or, in my case, drill) does not have to travel through the inside of the metal tailstock, so there is no risk of blunting the tip or damaging the tailstock. Also, extra reach is given, because the tailstock jig is only 55mm (2¼in) deep.

I use an old metalworkers' tap wrench to hold the long pattern drill.

If the workpiece is too long for a single boring process, I turn spigots and recesses for the three-way split ring at each end and reverse the piece once the first half has been bored.

In this case, the spigots would be 22mm (⅞in) to fit into both the PCC2000 centre boss and a corresponding recess in the tailstock jig.

C B Mather

Use a Pipe Cutter to Cut Ferrules

To mark a perfect square 90° around a small cylinder in readiness for sawing, I use a domestic water-pipe cutting wheel of the kind designed for cutting copper tubing.

Often, it becomes necessary to mark around a dowel, or brass tubing for a chisel handle ferrule, or copper tubing for the same purpose. For the cup lining of a candle holder it's better to use a hacksaw, as a pipe cutting wheel compresses quite a burr on the inside wall of the pipe, which then needs to be laboriously filed away with a rat-tailed file.

To clean up the cut end of a metal ferrule to remove any saw marks or rough edges, lightly jam it to the end of a tapered piece of wooden doweling, as copper tubing held against a sanding disc becomes too hot to handle in seconds.

Tony Evans

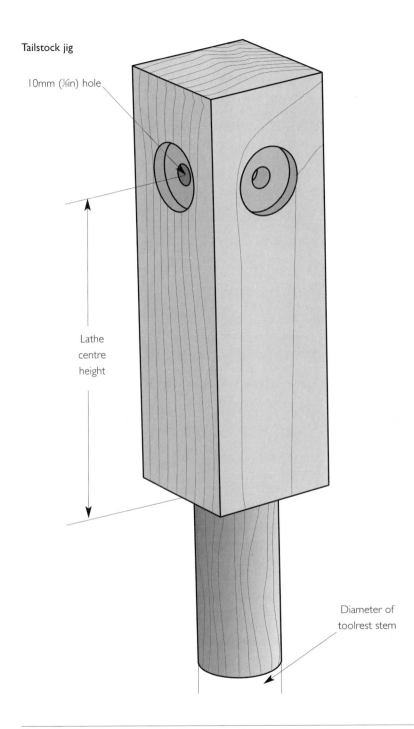

Tailstock jig

10mm (⅜in) hole

Lathe centre height

Diameter of toolrest stem

Pop Mark Helps When Re-chucking a Bowl

We all know the problems – such as of off centre loading and the bowl not cleaning up – when trying to re-turn a dried, wet-turned bowl.

Here is my method to ensure all surfaces 'clean up' and to get the bowl into balance. Faced with an oval, twisted bowl, the task often looks daunting.

Half the problem is solved if, when turning the dovetail recess to take a combination chuck in the wet blank, you only turn a ring out, instead of a recess, so that a pop mark – of say 8mm (⁵⁄₁₆in) diameter – can be turned in the centre, to match the tailstock point. This pop mark will stay amazingly central as the bowl dries and shrinks.

When, some months later, the bowl has dried out and is ready for re-turning, screw a piece of scrap wood bigger than the overall diameter (OD) of the bowl onto a faceplate and true up. Turn a recess into it, about 6mm (¼in) deep, to just accept the largest OD of the shrunken bowl. With the lathe switched off, the bowl can be carefully placed onto the faceplate recess and the tailstock brought up to fit into the pop mark.

The bowl's top edge will now need the high spots hand planed off, until about 50° of the top edge touches the faceplate, with no rocking to give a friction drive.

If the bowl is very oval, put woodscrews in the wooden faceplate on either side of the smallest width of the OD, to stop any sideways movement.

With the lathe on its lowest speed, turn out the ovality of the dovetail recess and true up the bottom. The bowl can now be mounted back onto the combination chuck and turned in the usual way. Keep the speed low until all surfaces have been trued and the bowl is in balance.

If you have several bowls to turn, start with the smallest, and then you can progressively open up the faceplate recess.

The main part of the tip is the pop mark – it really does work!

S A Tuck

Contact Glue for Bandings

In the past, when gluing narrow gauge bandings to the circumference of items such as goblets, stems of table lamps and small potpourri bowls, I found the end wouldn't stick and the banding would break during bending if I used glues like PVA. Now I use contact glue.

First, I measure the item's circumference, then cut a length of banding, allowing for handling and overlap. One side is coated with contact glue. The groove, previously cut, is also coated. When the glue has dried, the banding can be handled and bent into various shapes without breaking. It is now aligned, and pressed into the groove with a screwdriver.

When the two ends meet, the surplus is cut away to give a neat butt joint.

H C Crassfield

SETTING TOOLRESTS PARALLEL TO WORK

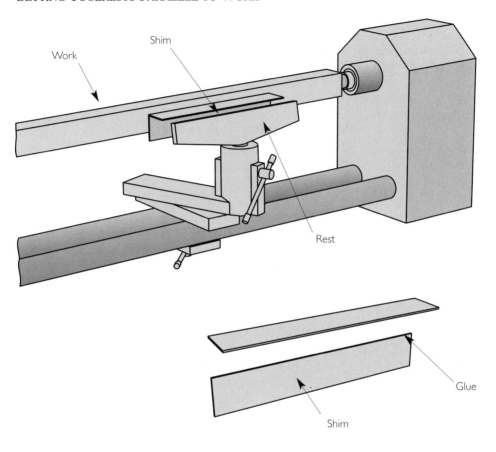

To keep your toolrest parallel to your work, place a plastic shim between the two. These are made from plastic offcuts obtained from double-glazing fitters, who are usually only too glad to get rid of them.

They come in different thicknesses, so choose ones to suit your tool use. Cut the plastic to the length of your toolrest and glue another piece on top at right angles. This will stop it slipping out when you adjust your rest.

In use, you clip the plastic shim over the toolrest and slide it into contact with the work all along its length. When you have tightened your toolrest and taken out the plastic shim, you will find the toolrest is parallel to the work throughout its length.

Turn the work by hand before starting the lathe, to ensure it clears the toolrest.

Peter Frow

Solving the Fluted Parting Tool Problem

The fluted parting tool's sharp corners can easily mark the toolrest and I have found it necessary to remove these marks quite often, as they affected the smooth sliding of other tools along the rest. Also, I tended to restrict my use of the fluted parting tool to situations where I wanted a certain size of groove with clean edges, or a bead.

One way of avoiding the problem is to glue a piece of wire of 2-2.5mm diameter in the flute of the tool, starting about 10mm (⅜in) back from the tip. I used a piece of welding wire, but copper would be just as good. Araldite fixes it well, and the wire can easily be removed for readjustment if needed. It will be a long time before sharpening reduces the length of the tool by 10mm (⅜in), as the illustration makes clear. I know of another turner who uses the fluted parting tool with the flute upwards.

Paul Smith

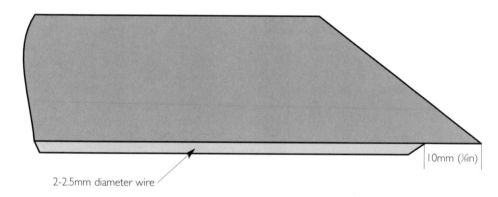

2-2.5mm diameter wire

10mm (⅜in)

The flute with wire in place

Using Wet and Dry Papers

As wet and dry papers are better used wet, but electricity and water don't mix, I use a wet sponge in a shallow plastic dish to wet the papers.

Just press them to the sponge and they will be wet enough.

J V Reilly

Use a Laser Pen to Align Headstock and Tailstock

I recently built myself a new lathe, on which the headstock can swivel around 360°. To align the headstock with the tailstock after a bowl-turning session, I use a small laser pen as used by lecturers and teachers. Buy a cheap one with a cylindrical housing and no clips or other attachments.

To align headstock and tailstock, mount a piece of scrap wood in a chuck, then turn or drill a hole with the same diameter as that of the laser pointer. Push the pen in the hole.

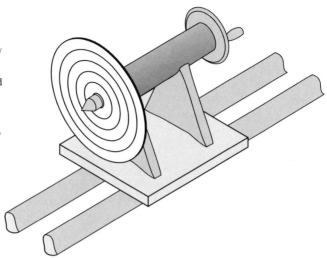

The target held in the tailstock

Cut a piece of cardboard, a circular target which fits tightly over the tailstock centre, the centre's point sticking through the target. Put the tailstock at the end of the bed.

Switch on the laser pointer (by putting sticking paper over the push button) and turn the spindle by hand. If the headstock is in perfect alignment with the tailstock you should see the pointer's red dot describe a circle around the point of the tail centre or, ever better, stay on the centre's point. If it doesn't, rotate the headstock until it is in line.

N.B. Don't ever look into the light coming from the laser pen, as it can damage your eyes.

Jan Hovens

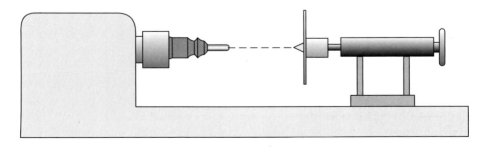

The laser pen held in its holder on the lathe

MAKE WINE STOPPERS WHICH FIT BOTTLES

I was disappointed with the couple of bottle stoppers I made as presents, because of their size and the poor quality of the corks. They looked like a pimple on a pig's back, as they did not fit the bottle.

I did manage to overcome this poor fit, however, provided the cork would take the treatment. As a wine maker I have to buy corks, but the top quality ones from Boots cost £1.05 for 12. So I decided to make my own.

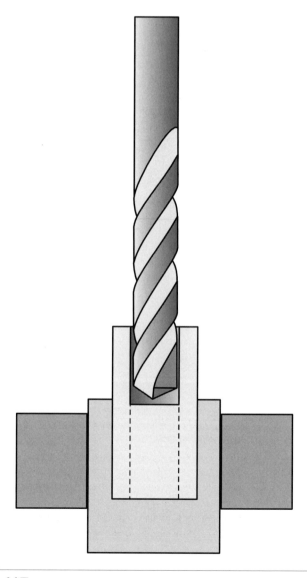

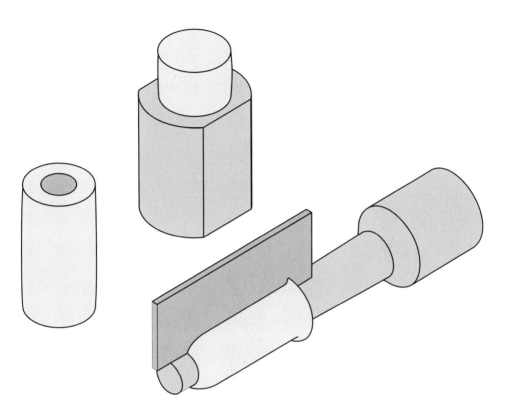

Take an oddment of wood, about 50 x 50mm (2 x 2in), the depth of a cork, and drill a hole to size, making sure the fit is tight enough to stop the cork turning under the drill.

Mark the centre of the cork and make a guide hole for the drill. Clamp the holder in a press vice, leaving clearance for the drill to go through the cork. I used a 12mm (approx. ½in) bit at high speed to produce a clean hole. Ensure the cork is vertical to the drill.

Cut the cork to an acceptable size for the lathe. From another oddment, turn a peg about 100 to 150mm (4 to 6in) long, of 10mm (⅜in) diameter at the end, tapering to 14mm (⁹⁄₁₆in). This will allow for any ready-made corks you may want to doctor.

Mount your cork on the peg and, with coarse sanding cloth, gently reduce it in size. It's useful to have an empty wine bottle handy, to get the best fit. Remember to leave a lip on the top of the cork.

Finish sanding the cork with a fine cloth before removing it from the stationary lathe, and cut it to the desired length.

Having made the ideal cork, make a ply or hardboard template for further use. You will now have wine stoppers which fit and can replace corks which are past their best.

Shaun Barbour

Chucks

MAKE YOUR OWN DOVETAIL JAWS

I am sure many readers have engineers' chucks they do not use to their full potential. With a little ingenuity they can make different sets of jaws.

First, obtain a set of soft jaws to suit your chuck. Mine is a Bernard three-jaw self-centring chuck. Tighten the jaws on to a 13mm (½in) shaft and mill or turn a dovetail slot. Make sure the jaws are numbered.

You can turn soft metal on a woodturning lathe – use the lowest speed possible and stout scraper tools with very light cuts. But, if you don't like the idea of hand-turning metal, a small engineering firm should be able to help, or make friends with a model engineer.

Turn the dovetail jaws from hard plastic or hardwood – plastic is easily turned by hand, using scrapers and low speed.

Mount the material for the jaws on the lathe and turn a disc to suit your chuck. The thickness of the disc for the jaws is the depth of the dovetail slot in the soft jaws plus about 13mm (½in), plus about 5mm (³⁄₁₆in) for the dovetail jaws you will be using to hold your woodturning.

Before you part the disc off, turn the dovetail to suit the dovetail slot cut in the soft jaws. And, assuming you are holding it in the relevant chuck, use the three-jaw positions to mark the 120° divisions on the disc face. Number the segments then part off the disc.

Place the disc in the vice, cut into three segments with a hacksaw, and clean up the saw cuts.

Put the soft jaws in the chuck, slide jaw segments into place with the dovetails engaged, then tighten (note they are self-centring).

You can now turn whatever shape jaws you need to suit your work.

Note there are no screws to get lost or nasty threads to cut your fingers while changing jaws, which is done in minutes. (*See illustrations on facing page.*)

You can make as many chucks as you need to suit the work under way and, for under £25, you have increased the versatility of items already owned.

D R Herbert

AN INNER TUBE CAN SAVE YOUR KNUCKLES

Newcomers can protect their knuckles from jaws projecting from the side of a four-jaw chuck with a band cut from a motorbike inner tube. This also stops the jaws dropping out if opened too much.

K W Vickers

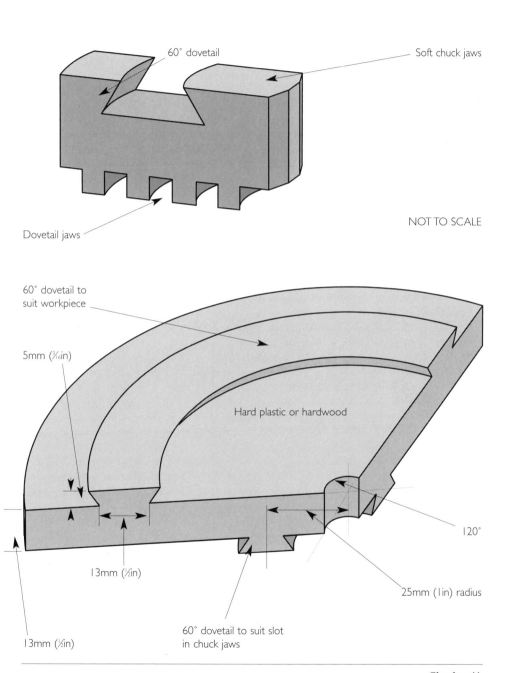

60° dovetail

Soft chuck jaws

Dovetail jaws

NOT TO SCALE

60° dovetail to
suit workpiece

5mm (³⁄₁₆in)

Hard plastic or hardwood

120°

13mm (½in)

25mm (1in) radius

13mm (½in)

60° dovetail to suit slot
in chuck jaws

HOLDING FINISHED WORK WITHOUT DAMAGE

I turn a lot of pots and find it time-consuming to make a jam chuck to finish the base. Ideally, I want my scroll chuck to hold the reversed work, but know the jaws would leave ugly marks whether gripping internally or externally, because the curve of the jaws is different to that of the items being held.

I have been using a Nova chuck with 50mm (2in) jaws, but the problem is similar with most scroll chucks. My solution is to use a length of rubber tubing, about 13mm (½in) diameter with a hollow core of about 6mm (¼in) diameter. This is slit down one side and can be fitted over the outer edge of the chuck jaws to provide grip and protection. A longer length of tubing can be used for items with larger diameters. The tubing can be obtained from car parts outlets. If there is a risk of damage to the top surface of the pot, masking tape or a leather disc will protect.

The grip works well inside or outside the item.

Bryan Hawkes

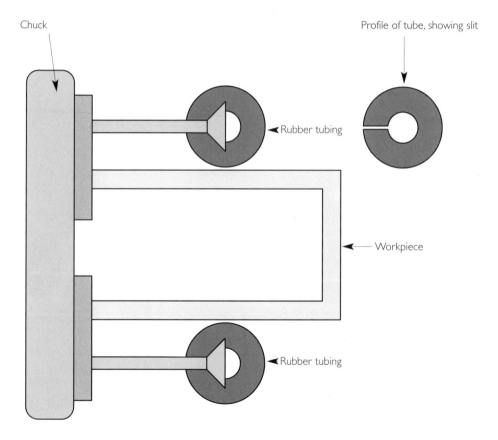

Preventing chuck jaws marking a workpiece

More Bite from Robot Mini Chuck Jaws

An operation a few years ago left me with no sense of touch in my left arm, making tailstock support essential when turning lace bobbins. But I found the square faces of the Robot Mini chuck jaws did not give a positive enough bite with the bobbin blank under pressure.

So I obtained a spare set of jaws from RTF Designs Ltd and, holding each jaw in turn in a small hand-vice, ground them to a profile similar to the jaws on a four-jaw engineering chuck. I left about 1mm (¾₄in) of the original jaw faces, which now bite into the hardest woods, as well as bone and Dymondwood. The modification also allows the jaws to close tighter than the 4mm (⁵⁄₃₂in) quoted in the specification.

Although I have no sense of touch in my hand, I still feel pain, and appreciate the Mini chuck's lack of protruding knuckle catchers.

Peter M Papworth

Protection Racket

The elasticated wrist and head bands used by tennis players make ideal protectors for the projecting jaws of 3- or 4-jaw chucks.

These jaws project beyond the main body of the chuck and, being invisible at high speed, are very dangerous and the cause of many accidents.

The brightly-coloured head or wrist bands (depending on the size of the chuck) make the jaws more visible and much safer. They make the difference between knocking your hand away rather than having a chunk taken out of it.

The bands can be obtained from most sports shops.

Tony Evans

Use for Hardwood Bungs

On the window ledge behind my lathe I keep a collection of turned hardwood bungs, about 3mm (⅛in) smaller in diameter than the maximum opening of the inside jaws. I glue them to work to be done on the lathe. By using Hot Stuff (cyanoacrylate adhesive) you can be turning in minutes.

On the inside end of the bung, I turn a smaller spigot, about 16-20mm (⅝-¾in) long and the same in diameter. The back register on my chuck is about 20mm (¾in). I have a flat spanner filed to this diameter to use as a gauge, and together with parting tool I can produce this small diameter spigot quickly and accurately.

The spigot should be slightly tapered at the end and be a good fit in the register. Adding the spigot greatly increases the rigidity of the job during turning and also helps re-centre the work if it has to be removed from the lathe.

When the turning is finished, part off and true up the end of the bung, making it slightly concave, and put aside for further use *(see illustrations on facing page)*.

K W Vickers

Releasing Work From a Jam Chuck

When jam chucking items for finishing, it's sometimes difficult to remove the finished workpiece from the jam chuck if the fit is tight, particularly if there is nothing much to get hold of. You can, of course, turn away the jam chuck, but there's always danger of contacting the work, causing irreparable damage.

If the jam chuck is held by a chuck or faceplate with a hole through it, drill a corresponding hole through the jam chuck. Before mounting the workpiece, which you will have already finished on the inside, pad the inside with tissue or rag.

When the time comes for removal, push a dowel through the lathe spindle and chuck to help free the workpiece. The tissue or rag will protect the finish.

Peter A Symonds

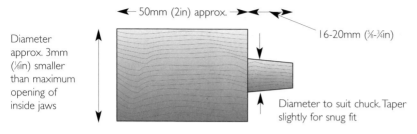

Diameter approx. 3mm (⅛in) smaller than maximum opening of inside jaws

50mm (2in) approx.

16-20mm (⅝-¾in)

Diameter to suit chuck. Taper slightly for snug fit

Hardwood bung

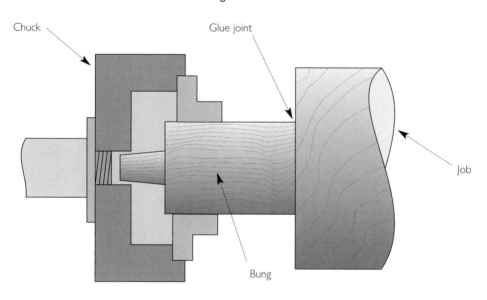

Chuck

Glue joint

Job

Bung

Chuck assembly

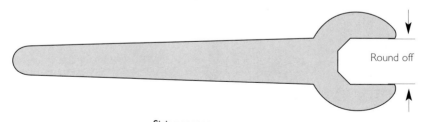

Round off

Sizing spanner

PROTECTION FROM THOSE FOUR-JAWS

I recently bought an Axminster Power Tools four-jaw chuck and, though very pleased with its performance, was conscious of the danger when the jaws protrude beyond the barrel.

I remembered reading a tip on using a section of car inner tube as a cover for the jaws, but thought this offered insufficient protection, so I came up with the idea shown.

To make it, I mounted a 150mm x 38mm (6 x 1½in) blank on a screw chuck, trued the face and the edge, and rounded the corners.

I marked circles of 135mm (5¼in) and 90mm (3½in) diameter on the face and hollowed between these to a depth of 32mm (1¼in) with a 3mm (⅛in) parting tool. Then I removed as much as possible of the remaining centre, down to the screw chuck.

After sanding and sealing I reversed the blank onto the four-jaw chuck, marked a 100mm (4in) circle, and cut through the 6mm (¼in) thick back to form a 100mm (4in) diameter hole (the size of the chuck body).

Make this a good tight fit onto the chuck – a layer of masking tape will help if it's too slack. With my new protector, I can now concentrate on my turning instead of on those jaws.

Les Jamieson

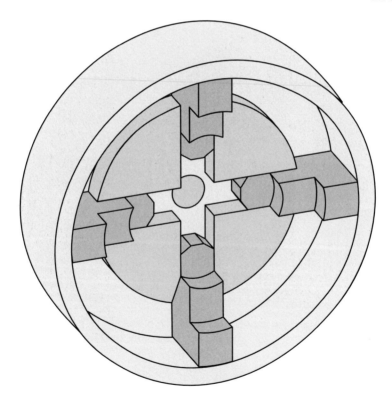

Protective sleeve for four-jaw chuck

Wooden Inserts for a Scroll Chuck

I make these inserts to give my chuck more versatility without buying expensive additional jaws. Being made of wood, you can work up to the edge without damaging your tools.

To make the wood inserts for a scroll chuck, cut a piece of scrap wood to fit the jaws at their most closed position. True up the face and drill a hole slightly smaller than the work you want to hold.

Remove the wood from the chuck and cut into four as shown, taking care to number the pieces first. Use an elastic band to hold the pieces together.

This wood insert can then be used for all diameters from the one you have drilled, up to about 8mm (⅜in) or more. For greater sizes, just make another insert.

To get a better hold, it's advisable to make the spigot diameter a little smaller than the work diameter. This forms a shoulder to set against the face of the insert and gives a better hold.

A Simmons

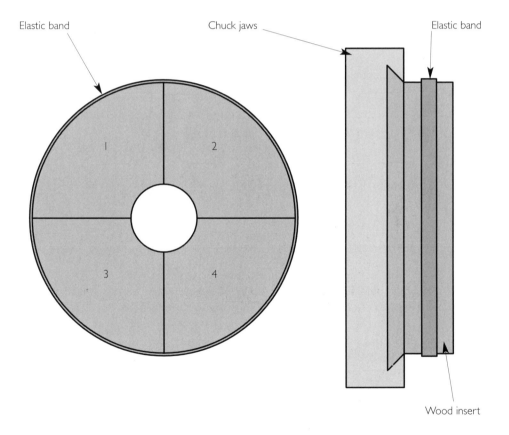

Inserts held together with elastic band

A 'STOPPER' FOR CHUCKS

My chuck stopper, for use on Child's 'Master' chucks or something similar, eliminates the need for a fiddly C spanner, and is very easy to use.

The metal band attaching the lever to the bed bar has a leather liner providing friction, so the lever can be left in any position.

When vertical, it is about 13mm (½in) behind and away from the chuck body, and can be pushed further away, even down to the bench, at the expense of being harder to reach. In any case, the lever is behind the chuck and usually out of the way.

The materials used were simply odd pieces from the scrap box, and the aluminium tube was taken from a sailing dinghy tiller extension (*see illustration on facing page*).

Robert McKerlie

CHUCKING PROBLEM

To overcome the difficulty of re-chucking a green wood blank into a dovetail expansive chuck, I leave a pillar around the pin-chuck in order to re-chuck onto the pin-chuck. This lets me reshape the dovetail recess, if necessary, when the wood dries out.

R Riseborough

SIMPLE BUT EFFECTIVE CHUCK CLEANING

Cleaning chucks is a tedious but necessary job, which can be made easier as follows. First, buy some surgical spirit (about £6 for 2 litres) from your chemist. Prepare the chuck by loosening the holding screws and place it in a polythene container. Cover the chuck with spirit and leave overnight.

Next day, swirl it round for a few moments in its bath. You will be amazed at the amount of debris which comes out. Drain and remove.

Using an old toothbrush suitably trimmed, get into all the nooks and crevices of your chuck. My Bonham has many!

Rotate the scroll ring at least one full circle to get into the difficult areas. Keep immersing the chuck in the spirit to remove stubborn particles. When satisfied it is clean, remove the chuck, drain off excess spirit, and dry with a rag or paper kitchen towels, because spirit dries quickly.

After a few times, the debris discolours the spirit, so filter it through a layer of kitchen towel. Lubricate the chuck, which is now ready for use.

Dr N De Netto

Chuck stopper

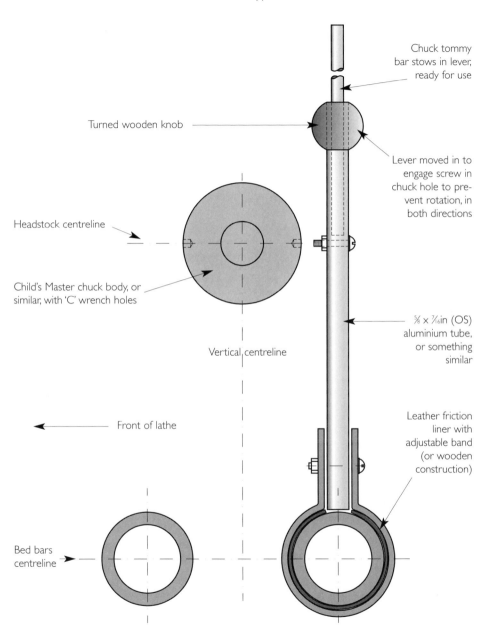

Chuck tommy bar stows in lever, ready for use

Turned wooden knob

Lever moved in to engage screw in chuck hole to prevent rotation, in both directions

Headstock centreline

Child's Master chuck body, or similar, with 'C' wrench holes

⅝ × ⅞in (OS) aluminium tube, or something similar

Vertical centreline

Front of lathe

Leather friction liner with adjustable band (or wooden construction)

Bed bars centreline

Axminster Access

I have had an Axminster four-jaw chuck for a couple of years and it is extremely versatile. When I remount rough-turned and dried bowls I reverse-mount them on a recess inside, then turn the outside. But the chuck key supplied cannot fit into the bowl to expand the jaws.

My solution is to get a universal joint from a socket-wrench set and fit a T-bar into it. The T-bar fits in the socket of the universal joint and the square drive shank fits in the chuck. I can now use the chuck inside bowls of 250mm (10in) diameter and more.

Glenn Lucas

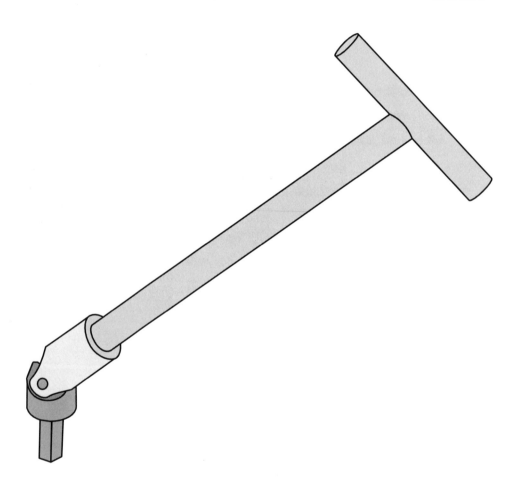

A chuck key made from a T-bar fitted in a universal joint from a socket-wrench set

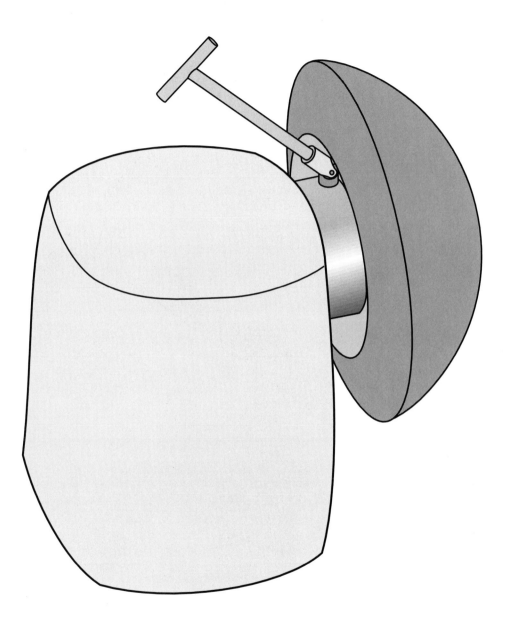

The chuck key in action inside a bowl. A chuck mounting is turned on the foot so the bowl can be remounted and the inside turned

A Chuck for Speedier Solitaire Plugs

The time it takes to make pegs for the game of Solitaire (to prevent marbles doing a runner) is brief, so there is a lot of stopping and starting. To speed operations, I made a chuck like the one shown.

I turned a piece of ash between centres and made a spigot that would cut its own thread into the unused thread of a 75mm (3in) faceplate. If you make this chuck, take care to see that the spigot does not bottom out before the two faces are brought together. Use the tailstock to keep alignment and a pipe wrench to get a tight fit.

This method also works well with larger end grain pieces. The chain wrench sold for the removal of oil filters works well with the bigger diameters. Turn the chuck to shape and to the size of the locking nut from a water pipe fitting. Again, use the thread to lock into the wood of the chuck.

Drill through the chuck for whatever size dowel you intend to use and make saw cuts. Remove the chuck with the faceplate from the lathe, clamp them in a drill vice and cut them on the bandsaw. In use, tighten the locking nut so that the chuck just grips the dowel. Make the first peg and cut off. Without stopping the lathe, knock the dowel through for the next peg. When it disappears into the headstock use a smaller dowel to push through. Trial and error will be needed to judge the total length that can be used – too long and it goes into orbit.

Gordon J Wicks

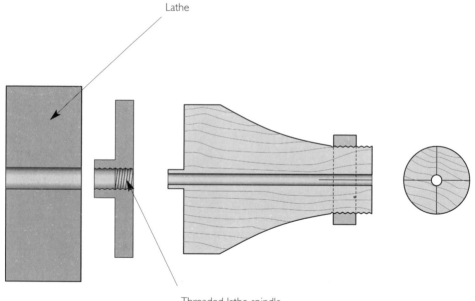

Lathe

Threaded lathe spindle

Chuck for making Solitaire plugs

A DEVICE FOR HOLDING SMALL BOWLS

I find this device very useful when turning small bowls and other smaller blanks which are difficult to hold. When used with small bowls it removes the need for the faceplate, and enables you to centre correctly every time. It is also ideal for ball tops, which can be screwed onto anything. On a 25mm (1in) dowel of hardwood, you can turn a 150 to 200mm (6 to 8in) bowl to a depth of 75mm (3in), as long as you have a good tight thread, a sharp tool and a light touch.

Thread cutters are widely available, cost about £25, and are very useful for many turning jobs.

J H Harris

13mm (½in) plywood disc with 25mm (1in) hole to protect chuck from chisel and hold the blank squarely and securely to the chuck

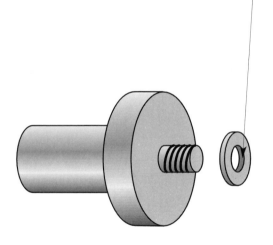

Chuck, male thread

Blank, female thread

BETTER GRIP WITH YOUR CHUCK

One of the problems with dovetail-type jaws found on scroll chucks is that there is rarely all-round contact with the dovetail spigot or recess.

In contraction on a spigot there are eight points of contact, which often leave irritating little 'L' marks on the work. In expansion the 'clover leaf effect' comes into play, with the centre of the outer edge of each jaw contacting the workpiece, giving four points of contact.

To get fuller exact and complete contact with a workpiece of a specific diameter there is a straightforward solution. It involves a four-jaw centring chuck, such as the Axminster, fitted with accessory mounting jaws and Axminster's Soft Top nylon jaws.

Open the nylon jaws to about mid-travel and fix them tightly in this position by clamping them to something of an appropriate diameter which wont get in the way. A two-pence coin is ideal!

Now turn whatever sizes of internal and external dovetail jaws you need. The nylon is very easy to turn. I used a scraper ground to 30° clearance angles and neutral rake, without a raised burr.

Because the new profiles will be perfectly circular at mid-travel this will give greater contact with the workpiece and prevent the bruising and marks sometimes associated with the standard jaws. It will also give a firmer grip.

Richard Prangnell

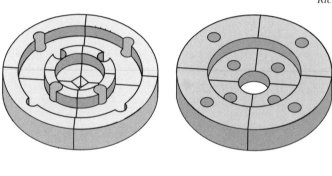

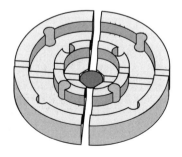
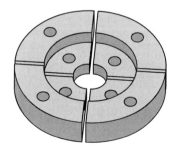

MAKE A BOTTLE STOPPER SCREW CHUCK

Many people try to turn bottle stoppers on the lathe by inserting a dowel into a blank, and holding it in a Jacob's chuck. Often the dowel breaks, and even when it doesn't, you have to sand the end of the cork and dowel flush.

I solved these shortcomings by buying a 13mm (½in) end-mill holder with a No 2 Morse taper, and milling a screw chuck out of 13mm (½in) bar stock. I cut a 75mm (3in) piece of bar and milled about 25mm (1in) down to 11mm (⁷⁄₁₆in).

Next, I cut threads for about 19mm (¾in) of the portion just milled and inserted the screw chuck into the end-mill holder until the front of the holder was flush with the point where the shaft stepped down from 13mm (½in) to 11mm (⁷⁄₁₆in).

I placed three 25mm (1in) diameter fibreglass washers over the shaft to prevent tool damage when cutting near the end-mill. I then drilled a 10mm (⅜in) hole in my blanks and threaded them on. You can easily turn the stoppers, with no danger of ruining the blank if you get a catch. The dowels can be pre-fitted into the corks, then later glued into the ⅜in hole in the stopper. Exact length is not necessary, as the short end will be hidden inside the stopper.

Kevin Miller

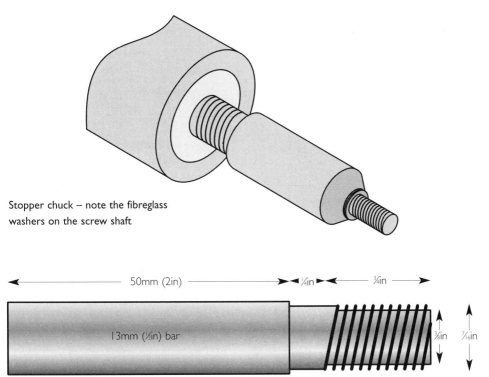

Stopper chuck – note the fibreglass
washers on the screw shaft

Bottle stopper screw chuck

HARDWOOD CUP FOR MORSE TAPER SPIGOT

A friend of mine had a problem with reverse fitting a half-turned bowl onto a chuck (in either dovetail recess or spigot mode) and getting it concentric without wasting time either making small adjustments or re-turning the bowl's outside lip.

His solution was to turn a cup in hardwood, on the end of a No. 2 Morse taper spigot (Fig. 1) with the cup a neat fit over the outside neck of the faceplate (Fig. 2).

After the outside of the bowl is turned, the faceplate is left on the workpiece and is held in a chuck in the tailstock. The piece is brought up to the chuck and tightened in place. The faceplate can then be removed and the inside turned out of the bowl.

Using this method, the workpiece is fastened virtually true each time. Should it not do so, check the alignment of the tailstock.

Ken Sager

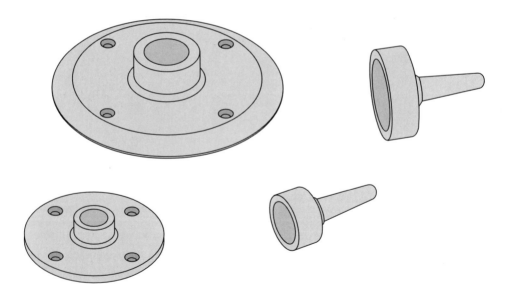

Fig 1: Hardwood cups to fit over the outside neck of the faceplates

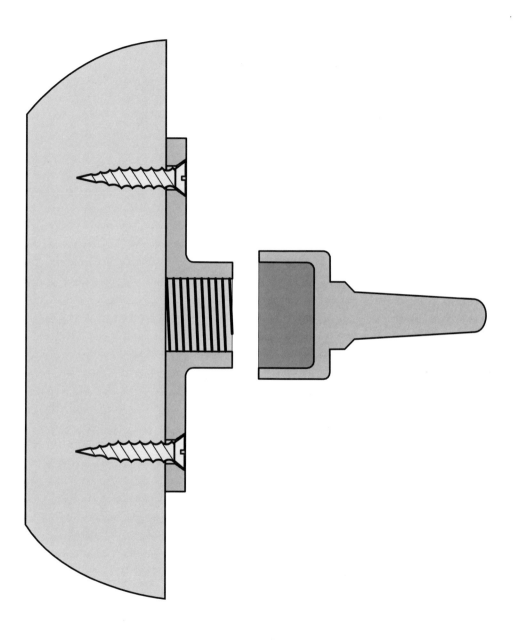

Fig 2: The set up on the lathe

WALKING STICK RUBBERS MAKE GOOD BUSHINGS

The idea for this tip came to me when I was recently turning a bowl from a big maple burl. I'd mounted the flat sawn surface on a faceplate and turned the outside shape, creating a foot or spigot to be gripped in my OneWay Stronghold chuck.

As with many burls, there were numerous cracks and bark inclusions, which I liberally treated with cyanoacrylate glue (Hot Stuff) as a precaution.

Once I was satisfied with the outside shape, I removed the burl from the faceplate and secured it in my chuck, ready to hollow the inside.

The grain was stunning and I tried to core out the centre, rather than waste it as shavings. Using the Stewart System slicer tool I began to core, but hit a bark inclusion. The tool jammed, causing the bowl to partially separate from the spigot still held in the chuck. Looking closer, I could see the spigot was weakened because of an internal bark inclusion and had separated along this fault.

Because the bowl's centre portion was now weakened by my coring attempt, I could not re-install the faceplate, and the spigot for the chuck was now ruined. It was head-scratching time.

Suddenly, I remembered my spouse's Christmas present – a set of jumbo jaws for my Stronghold chuck. But the bowl's weight and its incurved rim, meant the regular rubber buttons supplied with the jumbo jaws did not project high enough off the jaw plates and could not give enough gripping power. More head scratching.

Looking round my workshop I found a spare length of 25mm (1in) dowel, which I took to my radial arm saw and cut off eight pieces, 33mm (1⁵⁄₁₆in) long. I mounted each piece in my Nova chuck on the lathe and, using a Jacob's chuck mounted in the tailstock, counterbored and then drilled each length down the centre to take a suitably-threaded hex head machine bolt.

At the hardware store I bought eight of the rubber tips used for walking sticks (the largest size), which fitted snugly over the 1⁵⁄₁₆in lengths of 1in dowel bushing I'd already attached to the plates of the jumbo jaws with the countersunk machine bolts.

This idea helped me out of a difficult situation. I was able to turn away the damaged spigot and create instead a dovetail recess for the normal chuck jaws. Indeed it proved so successful in holding this heavy, unfinished bowl, that I had my local machine shop fabricate eight of these bushings from aluminium, to complement my jumbo jaws. As the rubber tips are available in different sizes, bushings can be created according to their size and the project you are undertaking. For safety, always bring up your tailstock live centre to provide light pressure and support when using this or any other form of jam chuck.

Kenneth R Goldspink

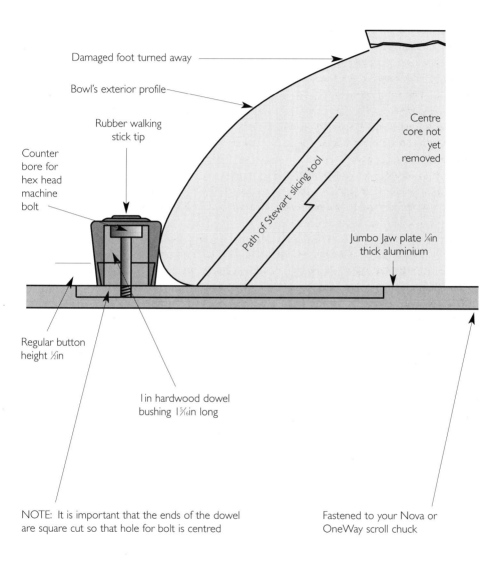

Damaged foot turned away

Bowl's exterior profile

Rubber walking stick tip

Counter bore for hex head machine bolt

Centre core not yet removed

Path of Stewart slicing tool

Jumbo Jaw plate ¼in thick aluminium

Regular button height ½in

1in hardwood dowel bushing 1⁵⁄₁₆in long

NOTE: It is important that the ends of the dowel are square cut so that hole for bolt is centred

Fastened to your Nova or OneWay scroll chuck

AN ECCENTRIC CHUCK WITH A DIFFERENCE

My X-centric chuck works differently from the commercial run-of-the-mill chucks. It allows eccentricity to be applied diametrically opposite, either side of centre, as well as indexing around the circumference of the article being turned.

The indexed chuck plate is divided into 12 indexed positions, and the indexed eccentric plate has 15. The centre three are blank, and the remainder marked from 0–5 on each side.

A slider block is dovetailed to the eccentric plate with a detent screw at its centre. This is to lock the slider block in any of the indexed positions right or left of the eccentric plate.

Two M5 countersunk screws mount the eccentric plate on the chuck plate. A variety of eccentric turnings can be produced by using a different combination of both indices.

Installation

The X-centric chuck can only be used with a self-centring four-jaw chuck. A sacrificial woodchuck is secured to the indexed chuck plate by four No 8 x 19mm ($\frac{3}{4}$in) long screws and turned true. While still on the lathe, a hole is drilled equal to the diameter of the screw chuck spindle, at dead centre.

Mark the edge of the wood chuck, at position 12 for example, so that it can be replaced exactly as before. Then remove from the chuck plate.

On the back of the woodchuck, chisel a square hole equal to the size and depth of the screw chuck head. Fit the screw chuck into the recess and replace the wood chuck on the plate, as before.

Select the amount of eccentricity needed by sliding the eccentric block to the indexed number, and tighten the detent screw. Place the device in the chuck jaws and tighten the chuck securely. The jaw faces will clamp the X-centric chuck on both edges of the eccentric plate and the slide block.

Operation

The first operation, whatever is being turned, is to turn it true. This is done with the eccentric plate located between the O marks and the tightened detent screw.

Decide on the amount of eccentricity needed by releasing the detent screw, moving the slide block to the required number left or right and re-tightening the detent screw as far as possible, to lock it.

To get clockwise or anti-clockwise eccentricity, the two M5 screws holding the eccentric plate to the chuck plate are removed and the plate set at 25mm (1in). The screws are then replaced.

This operation is repeated at one or more intervals, clockwise or anti-clockwise as required, until the article is finished.

To get exact opposite eccentricities, the slide block is moved from side to side (left to right) alternating between cuts. The detent screw is re-tightened each time at the same index number each side of the eccentric plate.

D G Ribbons

Right: The X-centric chuck. The indexed eccentric plate and the slide block are held in the jaws of a standard four-jaw chuck, the sides of both items being equal in width. The amount of eccentricity is set on the indexed chuck plate by screwing the detent screw through the slide block into the numbered recesses in the indexed eccentric plate. These are either side of the centre, so giving diametrically opposite eccentric working. The indexed chuck plate is indexed to 12 positions which would allow spiral eccentrics to be made. The screw chuck is held against the indexed plate by the wood chuck and becomes a simple screw chuck.

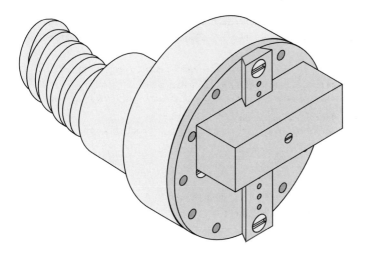

Left: The parts
fitted together with
eccentric turning

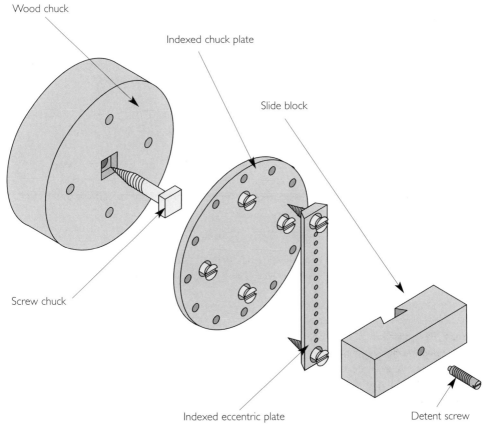

Wood chuck

Indexed chuck plate

Slide block

Screw chuck

Indexed eccentric plate

Detent screw

Storage

How to Find your Sandpaper

I overcame the problem of finding sandpaper among the shavings and sawdust on the lathe bench by putting the pieces in an open-weave basket about 200 x 100mm (8 x 4in).

A quick shake and the shavings disappear and your sandpaper can be found. It works even better if the backs are colour-coded.

J V Reilly

Storing Forstner Bits (1)

To protect the cutting edges of my Forstner bits, up to 30mm (1⅛in) in diameter, I store them in discarded plastic 35mm film containers.

I drill a suitable hole in the lid to take the shank, place the head of the bit in the container, slip the lid over the shank and clip into place. For larger sizes, I turn a spigot about 13mm (½in) larger in diameter than the head of the bit. Then, using the bit, I drill into the end of the spigot to the depth of the head and part off the spigot a little longer than the head.

Arthur Langtip

Storing Forstner Bits (2)

Use the following method to protect and store your Forstner bits. First, drill into a 25mm (1in) thick shelf with each drill bit, making a blind hole to the depth of the bit's body. Then drill out the centre of each hole to take the diameter of the shank of each bit.

Mount your shelf on the wall or in a cupboard and drop each Forstner bit into its relevant hole, upside down. Label each hole with the diameter of the bit.

To get to a drill bit, simply push the shank up and lift it out of its rack, returning it to the same place when you've finished with it. All my Forstner bits are now accessible, labelled and protected.

Dave Stephenson

Multiple Holder for Abrasives

I once stored in a drawer the excellent Hermes 406 I use as an abrasive for my turnings. There they tended to get mixed up with other items, making it a search to find the grade I wanted.

Now I use a kind of multiple toilet roll holder (see illustration), which is simply roll holders in a plywood box. Both sides are drilled for push-fit dowels, according to the number of abrasive grades in use – in my case five, with the coarsest grade at the top.

You just pull out the required length of the abrasive you need and cut it with an old pair of scissors kept handy.

Two 'key-holes' at the top of the fitment's back enable it to be easily removed from the wall for renewal of rolls. I've used this device for some time now, and find it saves a lot of time and frustration.

Tom Lack

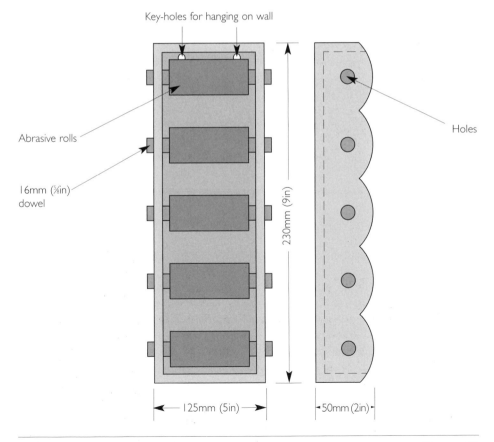

Key-holes for hanging on wall

Abrasive rolls

16mm (⅝in) dowel

230mm (9in)

125mm (5in)

Holes

50mm (2in)

AIRTIGHT STORAGE FOR BRUSHES

Having trouble with sanding sealer dissolving and brushes hardening? A cheap and simple device to solve this is to cut in half a one-pint square plastic milk bottle, with the cap left on.

After making 25mm (1in) long cuts in the top half, it will slide over the bottom half which contains the brushes, sealing off the air.

R W Smart

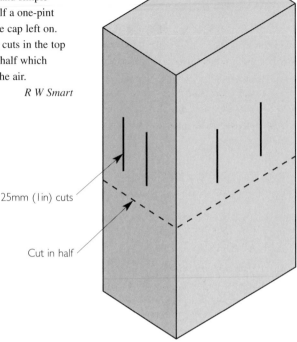

25mm (1in) cuts

Cut in half

KEEPING SANDING DISCS CLEAN

It's annoying, when you want to do some serious shaping with power disc sanders, to find your discs are in a pile of chippings with particles stuck to the velour. Even when you've removed them, you are not always sure what grit it is you have hold of.

My simple solution to this involves using strips of Velcro. I use 450mm (17¾in) self-adhesive lengths bought from Woolworths, and fasten these to any suitably-sized piece of wood, using one Velcro strip for each grade of grit.

Of course, you can only use the hook part of the Velcro, the same as it is on the pad of the sander. It's then an easy matter to remove and replace the discs you want, keeping the grits to their own row of Velcro.

Hang the wood panel somewhere out of the lathe's firing line and the discs will stay clean and ready for use.

How do you identify those grit grades in the first place, especially the white ones, which look much the same after use? Spend a few moments with a felt marker and write the grit grade on the velour of each one and you'll be able to read it for as long as the disc lasts.

Brian McIntosh

Storing Chisels and Preventing Rusting

I use washing machine waste pipe and water pipe insulation tube to store my woodturning chisels. It also keeps them rust-free.

I cut a 255mm (10in) length of piping, sliding the insulation tube inside the waste pipe. As a bottom to the pipe, I cut plastic circles of the same diameter and glue them in with superglue.

After mounting them on my workshop walls and inserting my chisels, the ferrule sits nicely on top of the insulation tube, leaving no gaps for rust to invade. (*See illustration, right.*)

S Gover

Storage Containers from Gas Piping

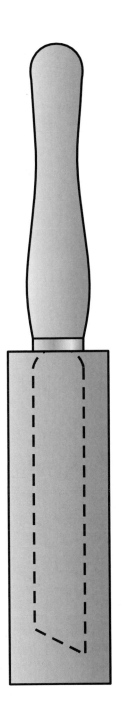

I made storage containers from some short lengths of 75 and 100mm (3 and 4in) gas service piping taken from a skip. The yellow pipes are made of polythene and have a thick 6mm (¼in) wall. Water service pipe is similar but coloured blue, and comes in even bigger diameters.

I cut the pipes into suitable lengths of about 125mm (5in) and supported them on the lathe with tapered wooden plugs held in the four-jaw scroll chuck and tailstock.

Trimming the ends square with a parting tool and skimming the outside with a scraper took just a few moments, the waste coming in a continuous ribbon off the scraper.

I turned a base and top from scrap hardwood, rebated to fit the tube. The base I pinned in place with brass pins in pre-drilled holes. The top had a small knob turned from the solid.

I use containers to store nails, pins, screws, chuck and small lathe parts. The blue water piping may be acceptable for kitchen use, but the yellow gas piping should, obviously, be reserved for the workshop.

Trevor Taylor

CORRUGATED TOOL RACKS

I have an Axminster M900 lathe, but this idea for a tool shelf and an angled tool holder could be adapted for any similar lathe stand.

The shelf and the tool holder are made with 6mm (¼in) plywood supporting corrugated PVC roofing plastic.

The lower shelf holds 8–12 tools which don't roll about or vibrate off the shelf because of the corrugated PVC.

The taper of the legs makes it impossible to insert a tight-fitting lower shelf in one piece, so it is cut in half and inserted one piece at a time. The plywood does not need extra bracing as it sits on the angle iron leg stretchers of the stand. The corrugated plastic is not fixed to the shelf, the weight of the tools holds it in place.

The upper tool holder keeps short-handled tools ready for use throughout a project. For longer handled tools, the tool holder needs to be at a shallower angle, or the handles get in the way during turning.

The dimensions of the upper tool holder are determined by the angle you decide to use. The lower edge sits on the back of the lower shelf. Decide how wide you want it, mark the position where the edge will come inside the front legs and use these marks to cut the shelf to size. Fix a 300mm (12in) wide length of corrugated plastic to the front of the tool holder before putting it in position. I have not fixed the tool holder, it is just slotted in and I have not had problems with vibration.

C B Mather

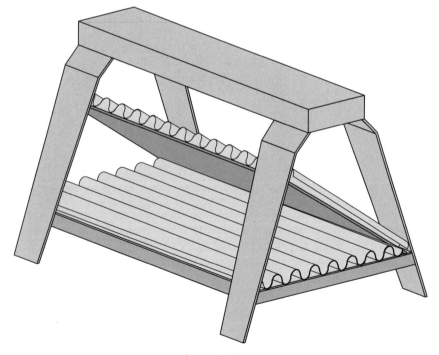

A completed rack

Use a Biscuit Tin to Store Sanding Discs

A simple way to keep power sanding discs in some sort of order is to utilise a biscuit tin with its plastic inner tray intact.

I was given a tin of biscuits with just the right size compartments for my discs and sanding pads. I have simply put the grit size on the top disc, but the compartments could be labelled in some other way. A nice way to make use of some packaging.

Terry Porter

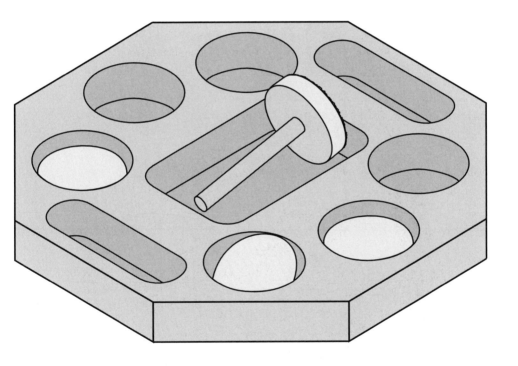

The biscuit tin's packaging makes a useful sanding disc store

A Magnetic Bowl for Metal Bits and Bobs

Some weeks ago I bought from my local car parts shop a magnetic bowl supplied by Draper for £3.50. It's made from strong, semi-rigid plastic with a powerful magnetic base enclosed in a rubber cover. I find this extremely useful for holding small metal parts such as grub screws, Allen keys, etc., especially the cutters of the Sorby RS200 and Stewart systems.

The bowl can be placed anywhere on the lathe and easily cleared of shavings by turning it upside down or blowing.

I now have several magnetic bowls around the workshop – they provide a home for 'bits and bobs' and have saved cutter blades etc. from loss in the shavings' pile.

Derek Green

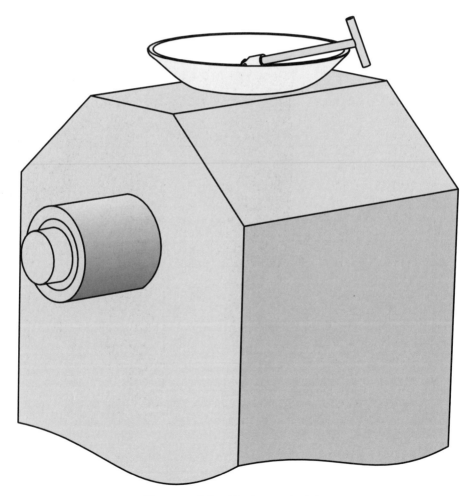

The magnetic bowl in place on the lathe

TIDY TOOL TOWER

Don't lose your chisels in the chips – use a tidy tower to keep them at your fingertips! To make one, take a 38mm (1½in) outside diameter steel pipe of a suitable length for your height. Mount this at the end of the lathe bed using angle iron drilled with holes to fit the mounting bolts on your lathe. If bolt holes are not available it may be necessary to drill and tap holes to match the tower base.

Thread the upper end of the pipe and fit a flange with three or four holes screwed on, to allow installation of the carousel. Use a square two-plate bearing (with the ball race between) for the top assembly. The upper metal plate is fixed to the underside of a 150mm (6in) square of 20mm (¾in) plywood, fastened to the flange at the top of the tower. The lower plate is fastened to the rotating tray.

The tray is made from 20mm (¾in) plywood, 330mm (13in) diameter. Drill holes at the outer edge to suit the size and type of your chisel handles (I turned the handles to complement the tray).

Cut an access hole of 100mm (4in) diameter in the rotating tray to let the pipe pass through, and suspend the tray from the ball race bearing. The holes are 6mm (¼in) in from the edge, and a section is removed to allow the handle to pass through and seat itself in the tray.

W Las

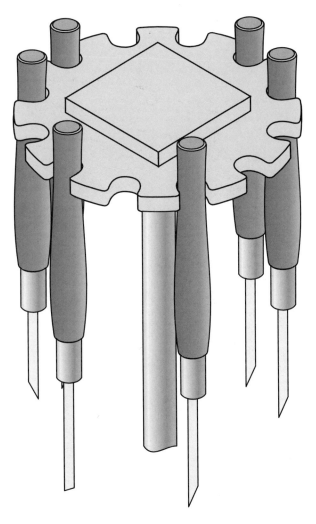

The tidy tower – a space-saving way to store chisels

Modifying and Improving Lathes

CHEAPLY MADE DUST-PIPE ADAPTERS

When using 110mm (4¼in) standard domestic soil pipe for dust extractors, there's always the problem of how to connect the 100mm (4in) flexible pipe to it.

Factory-made adapters can solve this problem, but they're not cheap (about £8.50 in the UK), so I came up with a much cheaper solution.

Axminster Power Tools sell for £2.93 a 110mm hose joiner (ref. no. HJ4), designed to connect with 100mm flexible pipes. It has a spigot at each end to fit inside the flexible pipe and a large diameter centre suction about 100mm long, which corresponds exactly with the internal diameter of the soil pipe. Cutting the joiner in half gives you two adapters for less than £1.50 each.

They can also be used to provide the spigot on shop-made dust cowls, simply by cutting a 110mm hole in the cowl and gluing in the adapter.

Phillip Ling

SWEET JAR USED AS EXTRACTOR HOOD

I've used a bell-mouth dust extractor hood on my lathe for the past three years. It is made from a 2kg plastic jar, obtained from a sweet shop.

The lid has a short thread, adapted as shown to take the size of the hose. I use a 100mm (4in) diameter hose. The jar is shaped to suit your set up – I usually remove the bottom.

This head has the following advantages over a purpose-made sheet metal extractor hood:
i) It's cheap; the plastic jars are usually thrown away by confectioners, and so there for the asking.
ii) The hood is rigid enough for the job, but unlikely to damage the workpiece or tools, should they accidentally hit it.
iii) Being light, the hood can be kept in position by fixing at the spigot end only.
iv) It can be easily removed when not needed.

After three years' use my hood shows little sign of wear but, should it need replacing, all I have to do is pay another visit to the sweet shop. (*See illustrations on facing page.*)

Harry Hobbs

Sweet jar dust extractor hood

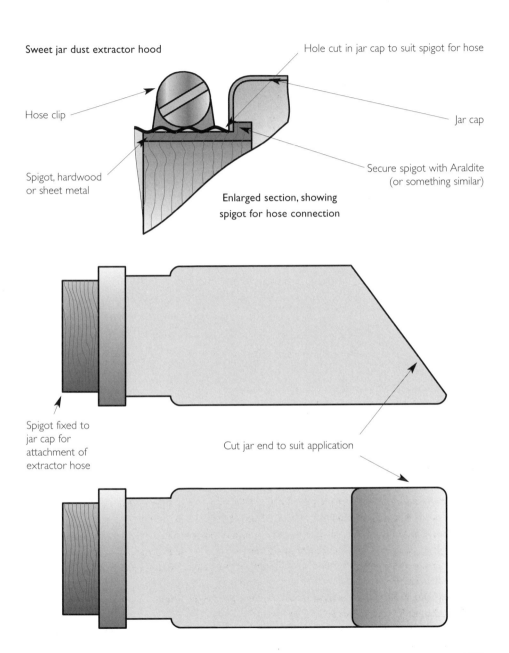

Hose clip

Spigot, hardwood
or sheet metal

Hole cut in jar cap to suit spigot for hose

Jar cap

Secure spigot with Araldite
(or something similar)

Enlarged section, showing
spigot for hose connection

Spigot fixed to
jar cap for
attachment of
extractor hose

Cut jar end to suit application

The sweet jar body is easily attached or removed from the hose connection by turning the hood 30°

Portable Bench for a Small Workshop

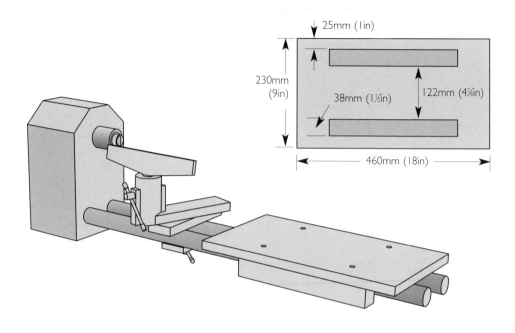

25mm (1in)

230mm (9in)

38mm (1½in)

122mm (4¾in)

460mm (18in)

The portable bench in place

As my workshop is small, yet contains a bandsaw, grinder, bench drill and lathe, I'm naturally short of bench space. To overcome this I have made a portable bench to fit neatly over the twin bed bars of my Record 24DML lathe.

Two 305mm (12in) lengths of 50 x 38mm (2 x 1½in) wood are screwed to a piece of 460 x 230 x 19mm (18 x 9 x ¾in) plywood. The first piece of wood is screwed 25mm (1in) from the edge, then the plywood is laid on the bed bars so that the other piece can be offered up to the board and marked. When this piece is screwed in place, it results in a snug push fit.

This firm, level surface is fitted in seconds, either between the head and tailstock or on the right-hand side of the lathe with the tailstock pushed forward.

The dimensions can be altered to suit individual needs, but I find this size handy for altering chucks on, or for such jobs as marking out.

George Capon

Nut Faceplate

I use a large nut, 38mm (1½in) x 6tpi, drilled and countersunk, as a small and very cheap faceplate on my Graduate lathe. You should be able to get one for about £1.20 from a good nut and bolt dealer.

Dave Wright

N.B. This is only suitable for light work – Ed.

Levering Device to Free Faceplate

Being unable to remove a 150mm (6in) faceplate from my CL2 lathe by the usual means, because it was so tight, I made the simple levering device shown. With it, the faceplate came loose with just a gentle nudge.

Peter Hallam

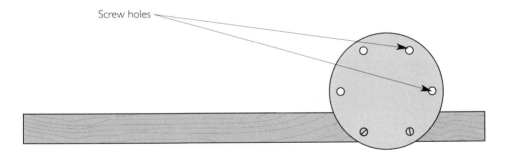

Screw holes

610 x 38 x 13mm
(24 x 1½ x ½in)

Device to lever a faceplate from the lathe

MODIFY YOUR TAIWANESE LATHE

I made an easy but effective modification to the fixing of the keyway strip on the single bed bar of my Taiwanese lathe, a WTL 12A. The keyway strip is on the underside of the bar, so many lathe users won't know that each separate piece is held in place by just three countersunk bolts.

This method of fixing allows considerable sideways movement of the keyway strip which, in turn, will permit unwanted backwards and forwards movement of the toolrest and tailstock, even when the locking levers are tightened. The amount of play in the strip can be seen and felt.

My modification involves adding extra bolts to attach the keyway strip more firmly to the bed bar. I added four equally-spaced countersunk bolts to each part of the bar, using appropriate drills and a 24 BSW tap.

For a few minutes of time well spent, you get a rigid toolrest and tailstock, greater accuracy and far less vibration at all speeds.

I think this simple modification could be made to all Taiwanese lathes which have a single bed tube.

J D Forder

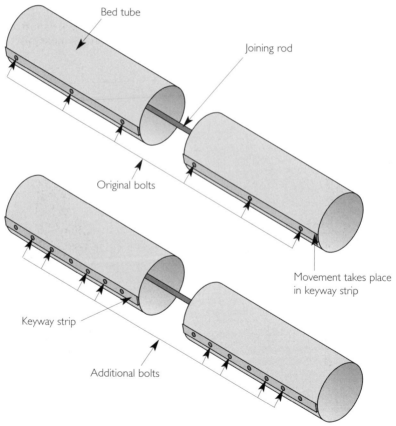

Bed tube

Joining rod

Original bolts

Movement takes place
in keyway strip

Keyway strip

Additional bolts

Extra bolts added for greater accuracy and less vibration

ADD WHEELS TO MAKE YOUR LATHE MOBILE

If, like me, you could always do with an extra bit of room in your workshop, then a few wheels can be of great help.

I have two lathes: a Graduate GL which certainly cannot be wheeled about, and a small Record lathe on a wooden stand. I do most of my turning on the Graduate, but do some small work and test small chucks etc. on the smaller lathe.

Consequently, the smaller lathe needs to be put out of the way at times. By following the idea of table saw manufacturers such as Kity, I decided to put some wheels on the smaller lathe.

This is really very easy to do. The wheels can be bought at any decent tool shop, and simply screwed or bolted to a firm structure to the outside of the legs at the headstock end of the stand. The wheels should be about 75 to 100mm (3 to 4in) in diameter, and be fixed, not swivelling. They should only just touch the floor when the lathe is in use, so the lathe is resting on the stand's legs and not the wheels.

To move the lathe about you just have to lift the stand at the lighter tailstock end until the wheels come into contact with the floor, and wheel it about. To make the moving even easier, pull-out handles could be fixed to the tailstock end and pulled out for better leverage and to save your back. The wheels cost about £8, and the support structure was made up from offcuts.

Terry Porter

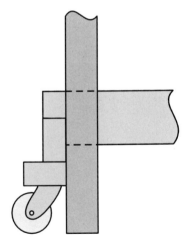 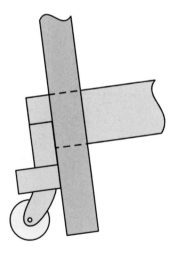

The wheels mounted outboard

TAILSTOCK DEPTH GAUGE

As with most lathes, my tailstock has no means of gauging depth when used for drilling. Since I'd been commissioned to make 100 items, each with a 12mm (½in) hole, to a depth of 30mm (1¼in), I decided to overcome this problem once and for all by making a depth gauge from odds and ends in the workshop, easily obtaining what I did not have from a DIY store. Few special tools were needed.

First I fixed an aluminium block to the side of the tailstock, straddling its centre line, having first ensured this positioning did not obstruct any access when turning between centres. (An alternative would be to use a short length of suitable angle in aluminium, steel or hardwood.)

I drilled a 7mm (%₂in) diameter hole through the block, the centre line of which is on the centre line of the tailstock barrel. This is to take the M6 screwed rod, which has to be long enough to accommodate the maximum extension of the tailstock barrel.

To determine the length of screwed rod required, first measure the maximum travel of the tailstock barrel, then add the thickness of the mounting block, plus the thickness of the M6 nuts, any washers, and the thickness of the pointer. In my case the tailstock barrel has a travel of 80mm (3⅛in) and the final length of screwed rod needed was 135mm (5¼in).

The pointer was cut from a plastic ice cream container to the shape shown, and painted red. It's located and firmly fixed at one end of the screwed rod simply by sandwiching it between two of the M6 nuts and washers.

A further M6 nut was then placed on the screwed rod and a washer added. The rod was put through the hole in the block on the tailstock side and first a washer, and then the final M6 nut, spun onto the screwed rod.

Find the datum point 2 (see Fig 1), for the end of the rod. Start by determining where your pointer datum point is (datum point 1). I used the end of the tailstock barrel and, with this fully retracted, offered the pointer to it. Fix the assembly firmly in place at this point by adjusting the nuts either side of the mounting block. The end of the screwed rod (furthest from the pointer end) is now your datum point 2.

At this point on the tailstock I engraved a line (an indent with a centre punch would also do). It's then simple to measure the depth needed, as the distance from the datum mark to the end of the rod will be equal to the drilling depth.

For easy reference, I also marked the drilling depth required for three items I make often (see Fig 2). These are simple engraved marks, each painted to stand out. I made a small, laminated sheet showing the marks and noting which item they refer to and the actual depth in millimetres. I pinned this to the workshop wall, just above the lathe.

In use, the pointer is positioned and the tailstock barrel fully retracted. The tailstock can then be moved into position with the drill bit or Forstner cutter just touching the item to be drilled (don't forget to allow for the length of the brad point etc. when setting the cutting depth) and locked into place.

Now drill the hole and, when the pointer is reached by the end of the barrel (or whatever datum point you've chosen), the hole is to the required depth and the drill is ready to be retracted from the work.

Richard Stapley

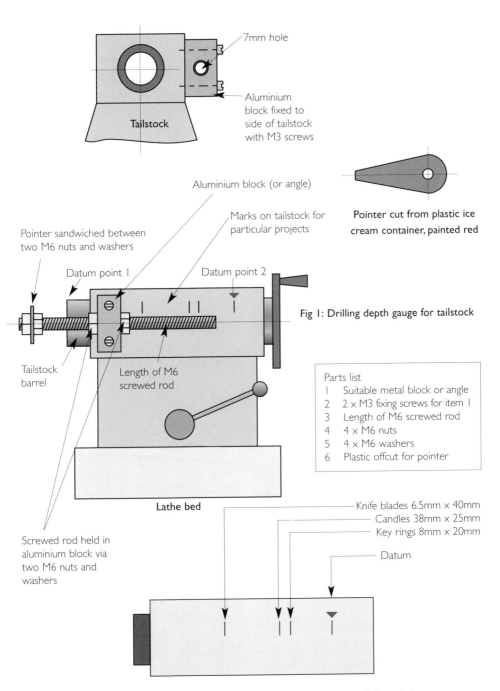

7mm hole

Aluminium block fixed to side of tailstock with M3 screws

Tailstock

Aluminium block (or angle)

Marks on tailstock for particular projects

Pointer cut from plastic ice cream container, painted red

Pointer sandwiched between two M6 nuts and washers

Datum point 1

Datum point 2

Fig 1: Drilling depth gauge for tailstock

Tailstock barrel

Length of M6 screwed rod

Parts list
1   Suitable metal block or angle
2   2 x M3 fixing screws for item 1
3   Length of M6 screwed rod
4   4 x M6 nuts
5   4 x M6 washers
6   Plastic offcut for pointer

Lathe bed

Screwed rod held in aluminium block via two M6 nuts and washers

Knife blades 6.5mm x 40mm
Candles 38mm x 25mm
Key rings 8mm x 20mm

Datum

Fig 2: Tailstock markings key on laminated sheet pinned to wall above lathe

ANOTHER TAILSTOCK DEPTH GAUGE

Richard Stapley's tailstock depth gauge (*see previous tip*) set me thinking about my own system. This is made up of a pointer (Fig 1) with two tool clips fixed to it (the clip size to fit tightly to the tailstock barrel). The depth gauge is a ruler, cut down and fixed to the tailstock (Fig 2).

I use the system to drill a hole to a set depth, mount the drill chuck, and drill and wind the tailstock up to the item to be drilled.

I set the pointer to zero by moving it along the barrel, drill the hole until the pointer shows the required depth, unwind the drill and re-check the zero setting. I repeat this if a new hole is needed.

The ruler is also useful for checking or setting callipers, etc.

A Garfield

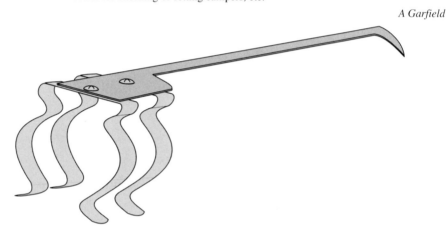

Fig 1: The pointer with two clips fixed to it

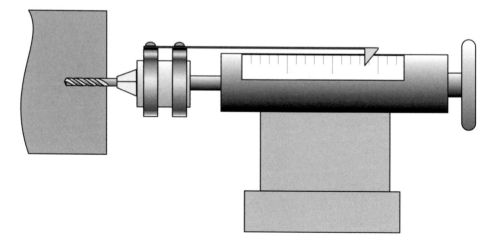

Fig 2: A ruler cut down and fixed to the tailstock

A HANDBRAKE FOR THE LATHE

It can be mildly irritating to have to wait for a fairly heavy workpiece to stop rotating on a lathe. A handbrake is the answer.

My Record Coronet No 2 came fitted with a machine screw incorporating an Allen key head at the left hand end of the drive spindle. It was a simple matter to turn a hardwood brake, shaped as shown, and fitted in place by the machine screw, a plate washer and split washer.

If, like my Record, the hole in the drive spindle has a right-hand thread, it's important to check that the handbrake is fitted very tight, or it can unscrew in your hand. Do this by tightening against a spanner on the spindle flat.

I have not included dimensions in the drawing, as these are best made to your own requirements.

A Devine

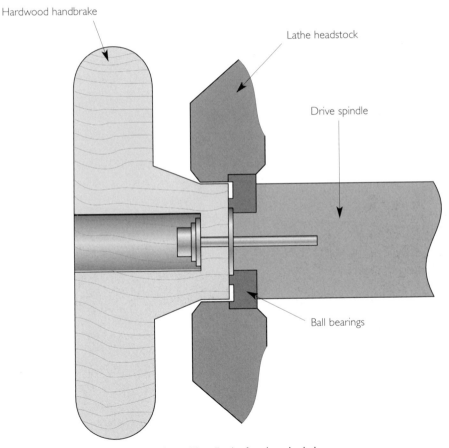

Hardwood handbrake

Lathe headstock

Drive spindle

Ball bearings

Hardwood handbrake fitted to the lathe

TAILSTOCK COLOURS TO MAKE BEARINGS SING

Like the life of most woodturners, a lathe's headstock bearing will last much longer if it is not forced to work for long periods under pressure. To avoid this, it must be tightened just enough to hold the workpiece securely and no more.

The downside is that the timber may, after a few minutes work, settle and loosen. You will then have to readjust the tailstock. The difficulty is in remembering to readjust in time.

Apply a little paint of a contrasting colour to one side of the live part of the tailstock centre (not white, as it dirties to the same colour as the steel). Anything from a beautifully painted half-and-half scheme to a splodge with a dirty brush will do.

With the lathe running, the colours and steel whirl together. Soon you'll find that without any conscious effort on your part, your third eye will give ample warning when the colour begins to change as the centre slows down. Adjustment is needed.

This method is simple, cheap and effective and, if you listen carefully, you will hear your headstock bearings singing their thanks for years to come.

Brian Hollett

G-CRAMP YOUR ROUTER TABLE TO LATHE BED BARS

If you are short of space in the workshop, then G-cramp your router table to the lathe bed bars (*see illustration below*).

The bed bars for my lathe, a DML 24 with 1150mm (45½in) between centres, are water barrel pipes from the local plumbers' merchant.

Ray Taylor

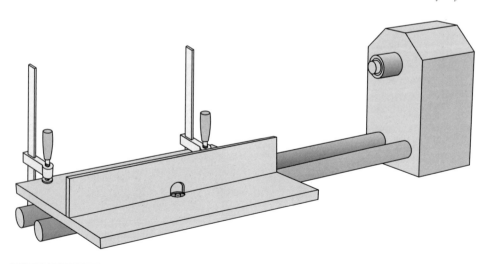

An Extra Hand to Support Work

When turning trays or other flat items, how many times have you needed an extra hand to support the work? Here's a project to give you that additional help, so you have full control of your chisels and support the work as well.

Using flat steel 38 x 6mm (1½ x ¼in), weld two pieces at right angles with a short connecting brace, as shown in the illustrations.

The length of each piece is determined by the length needed to mount it to your lathe bed. The upright must be long enough to allow for an adjustable arm of 75mm (3in) to reach the centre of the spindle.

The adjustable arm is made from a piece of steel 25 x 6mm (1 x ¼in), secured by a ⅜in bolt through the arm into a threaded hole in the supporting upright. When positioned, this bolt is tightened to maintain contact with the work.

The pressure wheel is an in-line skate wheel, mounted with a ¼in (6mm) bolt through the wheel into a threaded hole in the adjustable arm.

To position the pressure wheel to fit various diameters of work, the bottom piece of the support has a series of holes or a slot to allow the adjustment. If there is no suitable bolt in the existing bed mount, you may need to drill and tap a hole for this.

Walter Last and Doug Angus

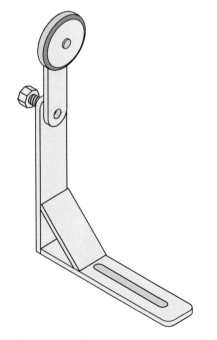

Two pieces of flat steel are welded together at right angles, with a short connecting brace

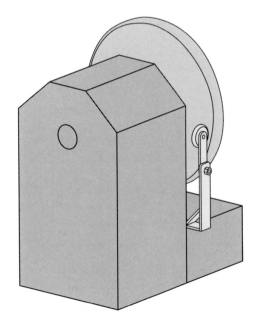

The pressure wheel in operation

Index

WOODWORKING

Toymaking

Designing & Making Wooden Toys	*Terry Kelly*
Fun to Make Wooden Toys & Games	*Jeff & Jennie Loader*
Making Board, Peg & Dice Games	*Jeff & Jennie Loader*
Making Wooden Toys & Games	*Jeff & Jennie Loader*
Restoring Rocking Horses	*Clive Green & Anthony Dew*
Scrollsaw Toy Projects	*Ivor Carlyle*
Scrollsaw Toys for All Ages	*Ivor Carlyle*
Wooden Toy Projects	*GMC Publications*

VIDEOS

Elliptical Turning	*David Springett*
Woodturning Wizardry	*David Springett*
Turning Between Centres: The Basics	*Dennis White*
Turning Bowls	*Dennis White*
Boxes, Goblets and Screw Threads	*Dennis White*
Novelties and Projects	*Dennis White*
Classic Profiles	*Dennis White*
Twists and Advanced Turning	*Dennis White*
Sharpening the Professional Way	*Jim Kingshott*
Sharpening Turning & Carving Tools	*Jim Kingshott*
Bowl Turning	*John Jordan*
Hollow Turning	*John Jordan*
Woodturning: A Foundation Course	*Keith Rowley*

MAGAZINES

WOODTURNING ◆ WOODCARVING ◆ FURNITURE & CABINETMAKING

THE DOLLS' HOUSE MAGAZINE ◆ CREATIVE CRAFTS FOR THE HOME

THE ROUTER ◆ THE SCROLLSAW ◆ BUSINESSMATTERS

WATER GARDENING

The above represents a selection of the titles currently published or scheduled to be published. All are available direct from the Publishers or through bookshops, newsagents and specialist retailers. To place an order, or to obtain a complete catalogue, contact:

GMC Publications,
Castle Place, 166 High Street, Lewes, East Sussex BN7 1XU, United Kingdom
Tel: 01273 488005 Fax: 01273 478606

Orders by credit card are accepted